LECTURES AND DISCOURSES-II

By

SWAMI VIVEKANANDA

Lectures And Discourses-II

By **Swami Vivekananda**

ISBN: 978-93-59393-46-9

Published by

DOUBLE 9 BOOKS

2/13-B, Ansari Road, Daryaganj
New Delhi – 110002
info@double9books.com
www.double9books.com
Tel. 011-40042856

This book is under public domain

ABOUT THE AUTHOR

Swami Vivekananda was born Narendranath Datta in India on January 12, 1863. He died on July 4, 1902, and was the most important student of the Indian saint Ramakrishna. He was an important part of bringing Vedanta and Yoga to the West. He is also charged with making people more aware of other religions and making Hinduism a major world religion. Vivekananda had a lot of success at the Parliament. In the years that followed, he gave hundreds of lectures across the United States, England, and Europe to spread the main ideas of Hinduism. He also started the Vedanta Society of New York and the Vedanta Society of San Francisco, which is now the Vedanta Society of Northern California. Both of these groups became the basis for Vedanta Societies in the West. Vivekananda was one of the most important philosophers and social reformers in India at the time. He was also one of the most successful and powerful Vedanta missionaries in the West.People now think of him as one of the most important people in modern India and Hinduism. Mahatma Gandhi said that after reading Vivekananda's works, he loved his country a thousand times more.

CONTENTS

The Ramayana

(Delivered at the Shakespeare Club, Pasadena, California, January 31, 1900)

There are two great epics in the Sanskrit language, which are very ancient. Of course, there are hundreds of other epic poems. The Sanskrit language and literature have been continued down to the present day, although, for more than two thousand years, it has ceased to be a spoken language. I am now going to speak to you of the two most ancient epics, called the Râmâyana and the Mahâbhârata. They embody the manners and customs, the state of society, civilisation, etc., of the ancient Indians. The oldest of these epics is called Ramayana, "The Life of Râma". There was some poetical literature before this — most of the Vedas, the sacred books of the Hindus, are written in a sort of metre — but this book is held by common consent in India as the very beginning of poetry.

The name of the poet or sage was Vâlmiki. Later on, a great many poetical stories were fastened upon that ancient poet; and subsequently, it became a very general practice to attribute to his authorship very many verses that were not his. Notwithstanding all these interpolations, it comes down to us as a very beautiful arrangement, without equal in the literatures of the world.

There was a young man that could not in any way support his family. He was strong and vigorous and, finally, became a highway robber; he attacked persons in the street and robbed them, and with that money he supported his father, mother, wife, and children. This went on continually, until one day a great saint called Nârada was passing by, and the robber attacked him. The sage asked the robber, "Why are you going to rob me? It is a great sin to rob human beings and kill them. What do you incur all this sin for?" The robber said, "Why, I want to support my family with this money." "Now", said the sage, "do you think that they take a share of your sin also?" "Certainly they do," replied the robber. "Very good," said the sage, "make me safe by tying me up here, while you go home and ask your people whether they will share your sin in the same way as they share the money you make." The man accordingly went to his father, and asked, "Father, do you know how I support you?" He answered, "No, I do not." "I am a robber, and I kill persons and rob them." "What! you do that, my son? Get away! You outcast! "He then went to his mother and asked her, "Mother, do you know how I support you?" "No," she replied. "Through robbery and murder." "How horrible it is!" cried the mother. "But, do you partake in my sin?" said the son. "Why should I? I never committed a robbery," answered the mother. Then, he went to his wife and questioned her, "Do you know how I maintain you all?" "No," she responded. "Why, I am a highwayman," he rejoined, "and for years have been robbing people; that is how I support and maintain you all. And what I now want to know is, whether you are ready to share in my sin." "By no means. You are my husband, and it is your duty to support me."

The eyes of the robber were opened. "That is the way of the world — even my nearest relatives, for whom I have been robbing, will not share in my destiny." He came back to the place where he had bound the sage, unfastened his bonds, fell at his feet, recounted everything and said, "Save me! What can I do?" The sage said, "Give up your present course of life. You see that none of your family really loves you, so give up all these delusions. They will share your prosperity; but the moment you have nothing, they will desert you. There is none who will share in your evil, but they will all share in your good. Therefore worship Him who alone stands by us whether we are doing good or evil. He never leaves us, for love never drags down, knows no barter, no selfishness."

Then the sage taught him how to worship. And this man left everything and went into a forest. There he went on praying and meditating until he forgot himself so entirely that the ants came and built ant-hills around him and he was quite unconscious of it. After many years had passed, a voice came saying, "Arise, O sage! " Thus aroused he exclaimed, "Sage? I am a robber!" "No more 'robber'," answered the voice, "a purified sage art thou. Thine old name is gone. But now, since thy meditation was so deep and great that thou didst not remark even the ant-hills which surrounded thee, henceforth, thy name shall be Valmiki — 'he that was born in the ant-hill'." So, he became a sage.

And this is how he became a poet. One day as this sage, Valmiki, was going to bathe in the holy river Ganga, he saw a pair of doves wheeling round and round, and kissing each other. The sage looked up and was pleased at the sight, but in a second an arrow whisked past him and killed the male dove. As the dove fell down on the ground, the female dove went on whirling round and round the dead body of its companion in grief. In a moment the poet became miserable, and looking round, he saw the hunter. "Thou art a wretch," he cried, "without the smallest mercy! Thy slaying hand would not even stop for love!" "What is this? What am I saying?" the poet thought to himself, "I have never spoken in this sort of way before."

And then a voice came: "Be not afraid. This is poetry that is coming out of your mouth. Write the life of Rama in poetic language for the benefit of the world." And that is how the poem first began. The first verse sprang out of pits from the mouth of Valmiki, the first poet. And it was after that, that he wrote the beautiful Ramayana, "The Life of Rama".

There was an ancient Indian town called Ayodhyâ — and it exists even in modern times. The province in which it is still located is called Oudh, and most of you may have noticed it in the map of India. That was the ancient Ayodhya. There, in ancient times, reigned a king called Dasharatha. He had three queens, but the king had not any children by them. And like good Hindus, the king and the queens, all went on pilgrimages fasting and praying, that they might have children and, in good time, four sons were born. The eldest of them was Rama.

Now, as it should be, these four brothers were thoroughly educated in all branches of learning. To avoid future quarrels there was in ancient India a custom for the king in his own lifetime to nominate his eldest son as his successor, the Yuvarâja, young king, as he is called.

Now, there was another king, called Janaka, and this king had a beautiful daughter named Sitâ. Sita was found in a field; she was a daughter of the Earth, and was born without parents. The word "Sita" in ancient Sanskrit means the furrow made by a plough. In the ancient mythology of India you will find persons born of one parent only, or persons born without parents, born of sacrificial fire, born in the field, and so on — dropped from the clouds as it were. All those sorts of miraculous birth were common in the mythological lore of India.

Sita, being the daughter of the Earth, was pure and immaculate. She was brought up by King Janaka. When she was of a marriageable age, the king wanted to find a suitable husband for her.

There was an ancient Indian custom called Svayamvara, by which the princesses used to choose husbands. A number of princes from different parts of the country were invited, and the princess in splendid array, with a garland in her hand, and accompanied by a crier who enumerated the distinctive claims of each of the royal suitors, would pass in the midst of those assembled before her, and select the prince she liked for her husband by throwing the garland of flowers round his neck. They would then be married with much pomp and grandeur.

There were numbers of princes who aspired for the hand of Sita; the test demanded on this occasion was the breaking of a huge bow, called Haradhanu. All the princes put forth all their strength to accomplish this feat, but failed. Finally, Rama took the mighty bow in his hands and with easy grace broke it in twain. Thus Sita selected Rama, the son of King Dasharatha for her husband, and they were wedded with great rejoicings. Then, Rama took his bride to his home, and his old father thought that the time was now come for him to retire and appoint Rama as Yuvaraja. Everything was accordingly made ready for the ceremony, and the whole country was jubilant over the affair, when the younger queen Kaikeyi was reminded by one of her maidservants of two promises made to her by the king long ago. At one time she had pleased the king very much, and he offered to grant her two boons: "Ask any two things in my power and I will grant them to you," said he, but she made no request then. She had forgotten all about it; but the evil-minded maidservant in her employ began to work upon her jealousy with regard to Rama being installed on the throne, and insinuated to her how nice it would be for her if her own son had succeeded the king, until the queen was almost mad with jealousy. Then the servant suggested to her to ask from the king the two promised boons: one would be that her own son Bharata should be placed on the throne, and the other, that Rama should be sent to the forest and be exiled for fourteen years.

Now, Rama was the life and soul of the old king and when this wicked request was made to him, he as a king felt he could not go back on his word. So he did not know what to do. But Rama came to the rescue and willingly offered to give up the throne and go into exile, so that his father might not be guilty of falsehood. So Rama went into exile for fourteen years, accompanied by his loving wife Sita and his devoted brother Lakshmana, who would on no account be parted from him.

The Aryans did not know who were the inhabitants of these wild forests. In those days the forest tribes they called "monkeys", and some of the so-called "monkeys", if unusually strong and powerful, were called "demons".

So, into the forest, inhabited by demons and monkeys, Rama, Lakshmana, and Sita went. When Sita had offered to accompany Rama, he exclaimed, "How can you, a princess, face hardships and accompany me into a forest full of unknown dangers!" But Sita replied, "Wherever Rama goes, there goes Sita. How can you talk of 'princess' and 'royal birth' to me? I go before you!" So, Sita went. And the younger brother, he also went with them. They penetrated far into the forest, until they reached the river Godâvari. On the banks of the river they built little cottages, and Rama and Lakshmana used to hunt deer and collect fruits. After they had lived thus for some time, one day there came a demon giantess. She was the sister of the giant king of Lanka (Ceylon). Roaming through the forest at will, she came across Rama, and seeing that he was a very handsome man, she fell in love with him at once. But Rama was the purest of men, and also he was a married man; so of course he could not return her love. In revenge, she went to her brother, the giant king, and told him all about the beautiful Sita, the wife of Rama.

Rama was the most powerful of mortals; there were no giants or demons or anybody else strong enough to conquer him. So, the giant king had to resort to subterfuge. He got hold of another giant who was a magician and changed him into a beautiful golden deer; and the deer went prancing round about the place where Rama lived, until Sita was fascinated by its beauty and asked Rama to go and capture the deer for her. Rama went into the forest to catch the deer, leaving his brother in charge of Sita. Then Lakshmana laid a circle of fire round the cottage, and he said to Sita, "Today I see something may befall you; and, therefore, I tell you not to go outside of this magic circle. Some danger may befall you if you do." In the meanwhile, Rama had pierced the magic deer with his arrow, and immediately the deer, changed into the form of a man, died.

Immediately, at the cottage was heard the voice of Rama, crying, "Oh, Lakshmana, come to my help!" and Sita said, "Lakshmana, go at once into the forest to help Rama! ""That is not Rama's voice," protested Lakshmana. But at the entreaties of Sita, Lakshmana had to go in search of Rama. As soon as he went away, the giant king, who had taken the form of a mendicant monk, stood at the gate and asked for alms. "Wait awhile," said Sita, "until my husband comes back and I will give you plentiful alms." "I cannot wait, good lady," said he, "I am very hungry, give me anything you have." At this, Sita, who had a few fruits in the cottage, brought them out. But the mendicant monk after many persuasions prevailed upon her to bring the alms to him, assuring her that she need have no fear as he was a holy person. So Sita came out of the magic circle, and immediately the seeming monk assumed his giant body, and grasping Sita in his arms he called his magic chariot, and putting her therein, he fled with the weeping Sita. Poor Sita! She was utterly helpless, nobody, was there to come to her aid. As the giant was carrying her away, she took off a few of the ornaments from her arms and at intervals dropped them to the grounds

She was taken by Râvana to his kingdom, Lanka, the island of Ceylon. He made peals to her to become his queen, and tempted her in many ways to accede to his request. But Sita who was chastity itself, would not even speak to the giant; and he to punish her, made her live under a tree, day and night, until she should consent to be his wife.

When Rama and Lakshmana returned to the cottage and found that Sita was not there, their grief knew no bounds. They could not imagine what had become of her. The two brothers went on, seeking, seeking everywhere for Sita, but could find no trace of her. After long searching, they came across a group of "monkeys", and in the midst of them was Hanumân, the "divine monkey". Hanuman, the best of the monkeys, became the most faithful servant of Rama and helped him in rescuing Sita, as we shall see later on. His devotion to Rama was so great that he is still worshipped by the Hindus as the ideal of a true servant of the Lord. You see, by the "monkeys" and "demons" are meant the aborigines of South India.

So, Rama, at last, fell in with these monkeys. They told him that they had seen flying through the sky a chariot, in which was seated a demon who was carrying away a most beautiful lady, and that she was weeping bitterly, and as the chariot passed over their heads she dropped one of her ornaments to attract their attention. Then they showed Rama the ornament. Lakshmana took up the ornament, and said, "I do not know whose ornament this is." Rama took it from him and recognised it at once, saying, "Yes, it is Sita's." Lakshmana could not recognise the ornament, because in India the wife of the elder brother was held in so much reverence that he had never looked upon the arms and the neck of Sita. So you see, as it was a necklace, he did not know whose it was. There is in this episode a touch of the old Indian custom. Then, the monkeys told Rama who this demon king was and where he lived, and then they all went to seek for him.

Now, the monkey-king Vâli and his younger brother Sugriva were then fighting amongst themselves for the kingdom. The younger brother was helped by Rama, and he regained the kingdom from Vali, who had driven him away; and he, in return, promised to help Rama. They searched the country all round, but could not find Sita. At last Hanuman leaped by one bound from the coast of India to the island of Ceylon, and there went looking all over Lanka for Sita, but nowhere could he find her.

You see, this giant king had conquered the gods, the men, in fact the whole world; and he had collected all the beautiful women and made them his concubines. So, Hanuman thought to himself, "Sita cannot be with them in the palace. She would rather die than be in such a place." So Hanuman went to seek for her elsewhere. At last, he found Sita under a tree, pale and thin, like the new moon that lies low in the horizon. Now Hanuman took the form of a little monkey and settled on the tree, and there he witnessed how giantesses sent by Ravana came and tried to frighten Sita into submission, but she would not even listen to the name of the giant king.

Then, Hanuman came nearer to Sita and told her how he became the messenger of Rama, who had sent him to find out where Sita was; and Hanuman showed to Sita the signet ring which Rama had given as a token for establishing his identity. He also informed her that as soon as Rama would know her whereabouts, he would come with an army and conquer the giant and recover her. However, he suggested to Sita that if she wished it, he would take her on his shoulders and could with one leap clear the ocean and get back to Rama. But Sita could not bear the idea, as she was chastity itself, and could not touch the body of any man except her husband. So, Sita remained where she was. But she gave him a jewel from her hair to carry to Rama; and with that Hanuman returned.

Learning everything about Sita from Hanuman, Rama collected an army, and with it marched towards the southernmost point of India. There Rama's monkeys built a huge bridge, called Setu-Bandha, connecting India with Ceylon. In very low water even now it is possible to cross from India to Ceylon over the sand-banks there.

Now Rama was God incarnate, otherwise, how could he have done all these things? He was an Incarnation of God, according to the Hindus. They in India believe him to be the seventh Incarnation of God.

The monkeys removed whole hills, placed them in the sea and covered them with stones and trees, thus making a huge embankment. A little squirrel, so it is said, was there rolling himself in the sand and running backwards and forwards on to the bridge and shaking himself. Thus in his small way he was working for the bridge of Rama by putting in sand. The monkeys laughed, for they were bringing whole mountains, whole forests, huge loads of sand for the bridge — so they laughed at the little squirrel rolling in the sand and then shaking himself. But Rama saw it and remarked: "Blessed be the little squirrel; he is doing his work to the best of his ability, and he is therefore quite as great as the greatest of you." Then he gently stroked the squirrel on the back, and the marks of Rama's fingers, running lengthways, are seen on the squirrel's back to this day.

Now, when the bridge was finished, the whole army of monkeys, led by Rama and his brother entered Ceylon. For several months afterwards tremendous war and bloodshed followed. At last, this demon king, Ravana, was conquered and killed; and his capital, with all the palaces and everything, which were entirely of solid gold, was taken. In far-away villages in the interior of India, when I tell them that I have been in Ceylon, the simple folk say, "There, as our books tell, the houses are built of gold." So, all these golden cities fell into the hands of Rama, who gave them over to Vibhishana, the younger brother of Ravana, and seated him on the throne in the place of his brother, as a return for the valuable services rendered by him to Rama during the war.

Then Rama with Sita and his followers left Lanka. But there ran a murmur among the followers. "The test! The test!" they cried, "Sita has not given the test that she was perfectly pure in Ravana's household " "Pure! she is chastity itself" exclaimed Rama. "Never mind! We want the test," persisted the people. Subsequently, a huge sacrificial fire was made ready, into which Sita had to plunge herself. Rama was in agony, thinking that Sita was lost; but in a moment, the God of fire himself appeared with a throne upon his head, and upon the throne was Sita. Then, there was universal rejoicing, and everybody was satisfied.

Early during the period of exile, Bharata, the younger brother had come and informed Rama, of the death of the old king and vehemently insisted on his occupying the throne. During Rama's exile Bharata would on no account ascend the throne and out of respect placed a pair of Rama's wooden shoes on it as a substitute for his brother. Then Rama returned to his capital, and by the common consent of his people he became the king of Ayodhya.

After Rama regained his kingdom, he took the necessary vows which in olden times the king had to take for the benefit of his people. The king was the slave of his people, and had to bow to public opinion, as we shall see later on. Rama passed a few years in happiness with Sita, when the people again began to murmur that Sita had been stolen by a demon and carried across the ocean. They were not satisfied with the former test and clamoured for another test, otherwise she must be banished.

In order to satisfy the demands of the people, Sita was banished, and left to live in the forest, where was the hermitage of the sage and poet Valmiki. The sage found poor Sita weeping and forlorn, and hearing her sad story, sheltered her in his Âshrama. Sita was expecting soon to become a mother, and she gave birth to twin boys. The poet never told the children who they were. He brought them up together in the Brahmachârin life. He then composed the poem known as Ramayana, set it to music, and dramatised it.

The drama, in India, was a very holy thing. Drama and music are themselves held to be religion. Any song — whether it be a love-song or otherwise — if one's whole soul is in that song, one attains salvation, one has nothing else to do. They say it leads to the same goal as meditation.

So, Valmiki dramatised "The Life of Rama", and taught Rama's two children how to recite and sing it.

There came a time when Rama was going to perform a huge sacrifice, or Yajna, such as the old kings used to celebrate. But no ceremony in India can be performed by a married man without his wife: he must have the wife with him, the Sahadharmini, the "co-religionist" — that is the expression for a wife. The Hindu householder has to perform hundreds of ceremonies, but not one can be duly performed according to the Shâstras, if he has not a wife to complement it with her part in it.

Now Rama's wife was not with him then, as she had been banished. So, the people asked him to marry again. But at this request Rama for the first time in his life stood against the people. He said, "This cannot be. My life is Sita's." So, as a substitute, a golden statue of Sita was made, in order that the; ceremony could be accomplished. They arranged even a dramatic entertainment, to enhance the religious feeling in this great festival. Valmiki, the great sage-poet, came with his pupils, Lava and Kusha, the unknown sons of Rama. A stage had been erected and everything was ready for the performance. Rama and his brothers attended with all his nobles and his people — a vast audience. Under the direction of Valmiki, the life of Rama was sung by Lava and Kusha, who fascinated the whole assembly by their charming voice and appearance. Poor Rama was nearly maddened, and when in the drama, the scene of Sita's exile came about, he did not know what to do. Then the sage said to him, "Do not be grieved, for I will show you Sita." Then Sita was brought upon the stage and Rama delighted to see his wife. All of a sudden, the old murmur arose: "The test! The test!" Poor Sita was so terribly overcome by the repeated cruel slight on her reputation that it was more than she could bear. She appealed to the gods to testify to her innocence, when the Earth opened and Sita exclaimed, "Here is the test", and vanished into the bosom of the Earth. The people were taken aback at this tragic end. And Rama was overwhelmed with grief.

A few days after Sita's disappearance, a messenger came to Rama from the gods, who intimated to him that his mission on earth was finished and he was to return to heaven. These tidings brought to him the recognition of his own real Self. He plunged into the waters of Sarayu, the mighty river that laved his capital, and joined Sita in the other world.

This is the great, ancient epic of India. Rama and Sita are the ideals of the Indian nation. All children, especially girls, worship Sita. The height of a woman's ambition is to be like Sita, the pure, the devoted, the all-suffering! When you study these characters, you can at once find out how different is the ideal in India from that of the West. For the race, Sita stands as the ideal of suffering. The West says, "Do! Show your power by doing." India says, "Show your power by suffering." The West has solved the problem of how much a man can have: India has solved the problem of how little a man can have. The two extremes, you see. Sita is typical of India — the idealised India. The question is not whether she ever lived, whether the story is history or not, we know that the ideal is there. There is no other Paurânika story that has so permeated the whole nation, so entered into its very life, and has so tingled in every drop of blood of the race, as this ideal of Sita. Sita is the name in India for everything that is good, pure and holy — everything that in woman we call womanly. If a priest has to bless a woman he says, "Be Sita!" If he blesses a child, he says "Be Sita!" They are all children of Sita, and are struggling to be Sita, the patient, the all-suffering, the ever-faithful, the ever-pure wife. Through all this suffering she experiences, there is not one harsh word against Rama. She takes it as her own duty, and performs her own part in it. Think of the terrible injustice of her being exiled to the forest! But Sita knows no bitterness. That is, again, the Indian ideal. Says the ancient Buddha, "When a man hurts you, and you turn back to hurt him, that would not cure the first injury; it would only create in the world one more wickedness." Sita was a true Indian by nature; she never returned injury.

Who knows which is the truer ideal? The apparent power and strength, as held in the West, or the fortitude in suffering, of the East?

The West says, "We minimise evil by conquering it." India says, "We destroy evil by suffering, until evil is nothing to us, it becomes positive enjoyment." Well, both are great ideals. Who knows which will survive in the long run? Who knows which attitude will really most benefit humanity? Who knows which will disarm and conquer animality? Will it be suffering, or doing?

In the meantime, let us not try to destroy each other's ideals. We are both intent upon the same work, which is the annihilation of evil. You take up your method; let us take up our method. Let us not destroy the ideal. I do not say to the West, "Take up our method." Certainly not. The goal is the same, but the methods can never be the same. And so, after hearing about the ideals of India, I hope that you will say in the same breath to India, "We know, the goal, the ideal, is all right for us both. You follow your own ideal. You follow your method in your own way, and Godspeed to you!" My message in life is to ask the East and West not to quarrel over different ideals, but to show them that the goal is the same in both cases, however opposite it may appear. As we wend our way through this mazy vale of life, let us bid each other Godspeed.

The Mahabharata

(Delivered at the Shakespeare Club, Pasadena, California, February 1, 1900)

The other epic about which I am going to speak to you this evening, is called the Mahâbhârata. It contains the story of a race descended from King Bharata, who was the son of Dushyanta and Shakuntalâ. Mahâ means great, and Bhârata means the descendants of Bharata, from whom India has derived its name, Bhârata. Mahabharata means Great India, or the story of the great descendants of Bharata. The scene of this epic is the ancient kingdom of the Kurus, and the story is based on the great war which took place between the Kurus and the Panchâlas. So the region of the quarrel is not very big. This epic is the most popular one in India; and it exercises the same authority in India as Homer's poems did over the Greeks. As ages went on, more and more matter was added to it, until it has become a huge book of about a hundred thousand couplets. All sorts of tales, legends and myths, philosophical treatises, scraps of history, and various discussions have been added to it from time to time, until it is a vast, gigantic mass of literature; and through it all runs the old, original story. The central story of the Mahabharata is of a war between two families of cousins, one family, called the Kauravas, the other the Pândavas — for the empire of India.

The Aryans came into India in small companies. Gradually, these tribes began to extend, until, at last, they became the undisputed rulers of India. and then arose this fight to gain the mastery, between two branches of the same family. Those of you who have studied the Gitâ know how the book opens with a description of the battlefield, with two armies arrayed one against the other. That is the war of the Mahabharata.

There were two brothers, sons of the emperor. The elder one was called Dhritarâshtra, and the other was called Pându. Dhritarashtra, the elder one, was born blind. According to Indian law, no blind, halt, maimed, consumptive, or any other constitutionally diseased person, can inherit. He can only get a maintenance. So, Dhritarashtra could not ascend the throne, though he was the elder son, and Pandu became the emperor.

Dhritarashtra had a hundred sons, and Pandu had only five. After the death of Pandu at an early age, Dhritarashtra became king of the Kurus and brought up the sons of Pandu along with his own children. When they grew up they were placed under the tutorship of the great priestwarrior, Drona, and were well trained in the various material arts and sciences befitting princes. The education of the princes being finished, Dhritarashtra put Yudhishthira, the eldest of the sons of Pandu, on the throne of his father. The sterling virtues of Yudhishthira and the valour and devotion of his other brothers aroused jealousies in the hearts of the sons of the blind king, and at the instigation of Duryodhana, the eldest of them, the five Pandava brothers were prevailed upon to visit Vâranâvata, on the plea of a religious festival that was being held there. There they were accommodated in a palace made under Duryodhana's instructions, of hemp, resin, and lac, and other inflammable materials, which were subsequently set fire to secretly. But the good Vidura, the step-brother of Dhritarashtra, having become cognisant of the evil intentions of Duryodhana and his party, had warned the Pandavas of the plot, and they managed to escape without anyone's knowledge. When the Kurus saw the house was reduced to ashes, they heaved a sigh of relief and thought all obstacles were now removed out of their path. Then the children of Dhritarashtra got hold of the kingdom. The five Pandava brothers had fled to the forest with their mother, Kunti. They lived there by begging, and went about in disguise giving themselves out as Brâhmana students. Many were the hardships and adventures they encountered in the wild forests, but their fortitude of mind, and strength, and valour made them conquer all dangers. So things went on until they came to hear of the approaching marriage of the princess of a neighbouring country.

I told you last night of the peculiar form of the ancient Indian marriage. It was called Svayamvara, that is, the choosing of the husband by the princess. A great gathering of princes and nobles assembled, amongst whom the princess would choose her husband. Preceded by her trumpeters and heralds she would approach, carrying a garland of flowers in her hand. At the throne of each candidate for her hand, the praises of that prince and all his great deeds in battle would be declared by the heralds. And when the princess decided which prince she desired to have for a husband, she would signify the fact by throwing the marriage-garland round his neck. Then the ceremony would turn into a wedding. King Drupada was a great king, king of the Panchalas, and his daughter, Draupadi, famed far and wide for her beauty and accomplishments, was going to choose a hero.

At a Svayamvara there was always a great feat of arms or something of the kind. On this occasion, a mark in the form of a fish was set up high in the sky; under that fish was a wheel with a hole in the centre, continually turning round, and beneath was a tub of water. A man looking at the reflection of the fish in the tub of water was asked to send an arrow and hit the eye of the fish through the Chakra or wheel, and he who succeeded would be married to the princess. Now, there came kings and princes from different parts of India, all anxious to win the hand of the princess, and one after another they tried their skill, and every one of them failed to hit the mark.

You know, there are four castes in India: the highest caste is that of the hereditary priest, the Brâhmana; next is the caste of the Kshatriya, composed of kings and fighters; next, the Vaishyas, the traders or businessmen, and then Shudras, the servants. Now, this princess was, of course, a Kshatriya, one of the second caste.

When all those princes failed in hitting the mark, then the son of King Drupada rose up in the midst of the court and said: "The Kshatriya, the king caste has failed; now the contest is open to the other castes. Let a Brahmana, even a Shudra, take part in it; whosoever hits the mark, marries Draupadi."

Among the Brahmanas were seated the five Pandava brothers. Arjuna, the third brother, was the hero of the bow. He arose and stepped forward. Now, Brahmanas as a caste are very quiet and rather timid people. According to the law, they must not touch a warlike weapon, they must not wield a sword, they must not go into any enterprise that is dangerous. Their life is one of contemplation, study, and control of the inner nature. Judge, therefore, how quiet and peaceable a people they are. When the Brahmanas saw this man get up, they thought this man was going to bring the wrath of the Kshatriyas upon them, and that they would all be killed. So they tried to dissuade him, but Arjuna did not listen to them, because he was a soldier. He lifted the bow in his hand, strung it without any effort, and drawing it, sent the arrow right through the wheel and hit the eye of the fish.

Then there was great jubilation. Draupadi, the princess, approached Arjuna and threw the beautiful garland of flowers over his head. But there arose a great cry among the princes, who could not bear the idea that this beautiful princess who was a Kshatriya should be won by a poor Brahmana, from among this huge assembly of kings and princes. So, they wanted to fight Arjuna and snatch her from him by force. The brothers had a tremendous fight with the warriors, but held their own, and carried off the bride in triumph.

The five brothers now returned home to Kunti with the princess. Brahmanas have to live by begging. So they, who lived as Brahmanas, used to go out, and what they got by begging they brought home and the mother divided it among them. Thus the five brothers, with the princess, came to the cottage where the mother lived. They shouted out to her jocosely, "Mother, we have brought home a most wonderful alms today." The mother replied, "Enjoy it in common, all of you, my children." Then the mother seeing the princess, exclaimed, "Oh! what have I said! It is a girl!"

But what could be done! The mother's word was spoken once for all. It must not be disregarded. The mother's words must be fulfilled. She could not be made to utter an untruth, as she never had done so. So Draupadi became the common wife of all the five brothers.

Now, you know, in every society there are stages of development. Behind this epic there is a wonderful glimpse of the ancient historic times. The author of the poem mentions the fact of the five brothers marrying the same woman, but he tries to gloss it over, to find an excuse and a cause for such an act: it was the mother's command, the mother sanctioned this strange betrothal, and so on. You know, in every nation there has been a certain stage in society that allowed polyandry — all the brothers of a family would marry one wife in common. Now, this was evidently a glimpse of the past polyandrous stage.

In the meantime, the brother of the princess was perplexed in his mind and thought: "Who are these people? Who is this man whom my sister is going to marry? They have not any chariots, horses, or anything. Why, they go on foot!" So he had followed them at a distance, and at night overheard their conversation and became fully convinced that they were really Kshatriyas. Then King Drupada came to know who they were and was greatly delighted.

Though at first much objection was raised, it was declared by Vyâsa that such a marriage was allowable for these princes, and it was permitted. So the king Drupada had to yield to this polyandrous marriage, and the princess was married to the five sons of Pandu.

Then the Pandavas lived in peace and prosperity and became more powerful every day. Though Duryodhana and his party conceived of fresh plots to destroy them, King Dhritarashtra was prevailed upon by the wise counsels of the elders to make peace with the Pandavas; and so he invited them home amidst the rejoicings of the people and gave them half of the kingdom. Then, the five brothers built for themselves a beautiful city, called Indraprastha, and extended their dominions, laying all the people under tribute to them. Then the eldest, Yudhishthira, in order to declare himself emperor over all the kings of ancient India, decided to perform a Râjasuya Yajna or Imperial Sacrifice, in which the conquered kings would have to come with tribute and swear allegiance, and help the performance of the sacrifice by personal services. Shri Krishna, who had become their friend and a relative, came to them and approved of the idea. But there alas one obstacle to its performance. A king, Jarâsandha by name, who intended to offer a sacrifice of a hundred kings, had eighty-six of them kept as captives with him. Shri Krishna counselled an attack on Jarasandha. So he, Bhima, and Arjuna challenged the king, who accepted the challenge and was finally conquered by Bhima after fourteen days, continuous wrestling. The captive kings were then set free.

Then the four younger brothers went out with armies on a conquering expedition, each in a different direction, and brought all the kings under subjection to Yudhishthira. Returning, they laid all the vast wealth they secured at the feet of the eldest brother to meet the expenses of the great sacrifice.

So, to this Rajasuya sacrifice all the liberated kings came, along with those conquered by the brothers, and rendered homage to Yudhishthira. King Dhritarashtra and his sons were also invited to come and take a share in the performance of the sacrifice. At the conclusion of the sacrifice, Yudhishthira was crowned emperor, and declared as lord paramount. This was the sowing of the future feud. Duryodhana came back from the sacrifice filled with jealousy against Yudhishthira, as their sovereignty and vast splendour and wealth were more than he could bear; and so he devised plans to effect their fall by guile, as he knew that to overcome them by force was beyond his power. This king, Yudhishthira, had the love of gambling, and he was challenged at an evil hour to play dice with Shakuni, the crafty gambler and the evil genius of Duryodhana. In ancient India, if a man of the military caste was challenged to fight, he must at any price accept the challenge to uphold his honour. And if he was challenged to play dice, it was a point of honour to play, and dishonourable to decline the challenge. King Yudhishthira, says the Epic, was the incarnation of all virtues. Even he, the great sage-king, had to accept the challenge. Shakuni and his party had made false dice. So Yudhishthira lost game after game, and stung with his losses, he went on with the fatal game, staking everything he had, and losing all, until all his possessions, his kingdom and everything, were lost. The last stage came when, under further challenge, he had no other resources left but to stake his brothers, and then himself, and last of all, the fair Draupadi, and lost all. Now they were completely at the mercy of the Kauravas, who cast all sorts of insults upon them, and subjected Draupadi to most inhuman treatment. At last through the intervention of the blind king, they got their liberty, and were asked to return home and rule their kingdom. But Duryodhana saw the danger and forced his father to allow one more throw of the dice in which the party which would lose, should retire to the forests for twelve years, and then live unrecognised in a city for one year; but if they were found out, the same term of exile should have to be undergone once again and then only the kingdom was to be restored to the exiled. This last game also Yudhishthira lost, and the five Pandava brothers retired to the forests with Draupadi, as homeless exiles. They lived in the forests and mountains for twelve years. There they performed many deeds of virtue and valour, and would go out now and then on a long round of pilgrimages, visiting many holy places. That part of the poem is very interesting and instructive, and various are the incidents, tales, and legends with which this part of the book is replete. There are in it beautiful and sublime stories of ancient India, religious and philosophical. Great sages came to see the brothers in their exile and narrated to them many telling stories of ancient India, so as to make them bear lightly the burden of their exile. One only I will relate to you here.

There was a king called Ashvapati. The king had a daughter, who was so good and beautiful that she was called Sâvitri, which is the name of a sacred prayer of the Hindus. When Savitri grew old enough, her father asked her to choose a husband for herself. These ancient Indian princesses were very independent, you see, and chose their own princely suitors.

Savitri consented and travelled in distant regions, mounted in a golden chariot, with her guards and aged courtiers to whom her father entrusted her, stopping at different courts, and seeing different princes, but not one of them could win the heart of Savitri. They came at last to a holy hermitage in one of those forests that in ancient India were reserved for animals, and where no animals were allowed to be killed. The animals lost the fear of man — even the fish in the lakes came and took food out of the hand. For thousands of years no one had killed anything therein. The sages and the aged went there to live among the deer and the birds. Even criminals were safe there. When a man got tired of life, he would go to the forest; and in the company of sages, talking of religion and meditating thereon, he passed the remainder of his life.

Now it happened that there was a king, Dyumatsena, who was defeated by his enemies and was deprived of his kingdom when he was struck with age and had lost his sight. This poor, old, blind king, with his queen and his son, took refuge in the forest and passed his life in rigid penance. His boy's name was Satyavân.

It came to pass that after having visited all the different royal courts, Savitri at last came to this hermitage, or holy place. Not even the greatest king could pass by the hermitages, or Âshramas as they were called, without going to pay homage to the sages, for such honour and respect was felt for these holy men. The greatest emperor of India would be only too glad to trace his descent to some sage who lived in a forest, subsisting on roots and fruits, and clad in rags. We are all children of sages. That is the respect that is paid to religion. So, even kings, when they pass by the hermitages, feel honoured to go in and pay their respects to the sages. If they approach on horseback, they descend and walk as they advance towards them. If they arrive in a chariot, chariot and armour must be left outside when they enter.

No fighting man can enter unless he comes in the manner of a religious man, quiet and gentle.

So Savitri came to this hermitage and saw there Satyavan, the hermit's son, and her heart was conquered. She had escaped all the princes of the palaces and the courts, but here in the forest-refuge of King Dyumatsena, his son, Satyavan, stole her heart.

When Savitri returned to her father's house, he asked her, "Savitri, dear daughter, speak. Did you see anybody whom you would like to marry ?" Then softly with blushes, said Savitri, "Yes, father." "What is the name of the prince?" "He is no prince, but the son of King Dyumatsena who has lost his kingdom — a prince without a patrimony, who lives a monastic life, the life of a Sannyasin in a forest, collecting roots and herbs, helping and feeding his old father and mother, who live in a cottage."

On hearing this the father consulted the Sage Nârada, who happened to be then present there, and he declared it was the most ill-omened choice that was ever made. The king then asked him to explain why it was so. And Narada said, "Within twelve months from this time the young man will die." Then the king started with terror, and spoke, "Savitri, this young man is going to die in twelve months, and you will become a widow: think of that! Desist from your choice, my child, you shall never be married to a short-lived and fated bridegroom." "Never mind, father; do not ask me to marry another person and sacrifice the chastity of mind, for I love and have accepted in my mind that good and brave Satyavan only as my husband. A maiden chooses only once, and she never departs from her troth." When the king found that Savitri was resolute in mind and heart, he complied. Then Savitri married prince Satyavan, and she quietly went from the palace of her father into the forest, to live with her chosen husband and help her husband's parents. Now, though Savitri knew the exact date when Satyavan was to die, she kept it hidden from him. Daily he went into the depths of the forest, collected fruits and flowers, gathered faggots, and then came back to the cottage, and she cooked the meals and helped the old people. Thus their lives went on until the fatal day came near, and three short days remained only. She took a severe vow of three nights' penance and holy fasts, and kept her hard vigils. Savitri spent sorrowful and sleepless nights with fervent prayers and unseen tears, till the dreaded morning dawned. That day Savitri could not bear him out of her sight, even for a moment. She begged permission from his parents to accompany her husband, when he went to gather the usual herbs and fuel, and gaining their consent she went. Suddenly, in faltering accents, he complained to his wife of feeling faint, "My head is dizzy, and my senses reel, dear Savitri, I feel sleep stealing over me; let me rest beside thee for a while." In fear and trembling she replied, "Come, lay your head upon my lap, my dearest lord." And he laid his burning head in the lap of his wife, and ere long sighed and expired. Clasping him to her, her eyes flowing with tears, there she sat in the lonesome forest, until the emissaries of Death approached to take away the soul of Satyavan. But they could not come near to the place where Savitri sat with the dead body of her husband, his head resting in her lap. There was a zone of fire surrounding her, and not one of the emissaries of Death could come within it. They all fled back from it, returned to King Yama, the God of Death, and told him why they could not obtain the soul of this man.

Then came Yama, the God of Death, the Judge of the dead. He was the first man that died — the first man that died on earth — and he had become the presiding deity over all those that die. He judges whether, after a man has died, he is to be punished or rewarded. So he came himself. Of course, he could go inside that charmed circle as he was a god. When he came to Savitri, he said, "Daughter, give up this dead body, for know, death is the fate of mortals, and I am the first of mortals who died. Since then, everyone has had to die. Death is the fate of man." Thus told, Savitri walked off, and Yama drew the soul out. Yama having possessed himself of the soul of the young man proceeded on his way. Before he had gone far, he heard footfalls upon the dry leaves. He turned back. "Savitri, daughter, why are you following me? This is the fate of all mortals." "I am not following thee, Father," replied Savitri, "but this is, also, the fate of woman, she follows where her love takes her, and the Eternal Law separates not loving man and faithful wife." Then said the God of Death, "Ask for any boon, except the life of your husband." "If thou art pleased to grant a boon, O Lord of Death, I ask that my father-in-law may be cured of his blindness and made happy." "Let thy pious wish be granted, duteous daughter." And then the King of Death travelled on with the soul of Satyavan. Again the same footfall was heard from behind. He looked round. "Savitri, my daughter, you are still following me?" "Yes my Father; I cannot help doing so; I am trying all the time to go back, but the mind goes after my husband and the body follows. The soul has already gone, for in that soul is also mine; and when you take the soul, the body follows, does it not?" "Pleased am I with your words, fair Savitri. Ask yet another boon of me, but it must not be the life of your husband." "Let my father-in-law regain his lost wealth and kingdom, Father, if thou art pleased to grant another supplication." "Loving daughter," Yama answered, "this boon I now bestow; but return home, for living mortal cannot go with King Yama." And then Yama pursued his way. But Savitri, meek and faithful still followed her departed husband. Yama again turned back. "Noble Savitri, follow not in hopeless woe." "I cannot choose but follow where thou takest my beloved one." "Then suppose, Savitri, that your husband was a sinner and has to go to hell. In that case goes Savitri with the one she loves?" "Glad am I to follow where he goes be it life or death, heaven or hell," said the loving wife. "Blessed are your words, my child, pleased am I with you, ask yet another boon, but the dead come not to life again." "Since you so permit me, then, let the imperial line of my father-in-law be not destroyed; let his kingdom descend to Satyavan's sons." And then the God of Death smiled. "My daughter, thou shalt have thy desire now: here is the soul of thy husband, he shall live again. He shall live to be a father and thy children also shall reign in due course. Return home. Love has conquered Death! Woman never loved like thee, and thou art the proof that even I, the God of Death, am powerless against the power of the true love that abideth!"

This is the story of Savitri, and every girl in India must aspire to be like Savitri, whose love could not be conquered by death, and who through this tremendous love snatched back from even Yama, the soul of her husband.

The book is full of hundreds of beautiful episodes like this. I began by telling you that the Mahabharata is one of the greatest books in the world and consists of about a hundred thousand verses in eighteen Parvans, or volumes.

To return to our main story. We left the Pandava brothers in exile. Even there they were not allowed to remain unmolested from the evil plots of Duryodhana; but all of them were futile.

A story of their forest life, I shall tell you here. One day the brothers became thirsty in the forest. Yudhishthira bade his brother, Nakula, go and fetch water. He quickly proceeded towards the place where there was water and soon came to a crystal lake, and was about to drink of it, when he heard a voice utter these words: "Stop, O child. First answer my questions and then drink of this water." But Nakula, who was exceedingly thirsty, disregarded these words, drank of the water, and having drunk of it, dropped down dead. As Nakula did not return, King Yudhishthira told Sahadeva to seek his brother and bring back water with him. So Sahadeva proceeded to the lake and beheld his brother lying dead. Afflicted at the death of his brother and suffering severely from thirst, he went towards the water, when the same words were heard by him: "O child, first answer my questions and then drink of the water." He also disregarded these words, and having satisfied his thirst, dropped down dead. Subsequently, Arjuna and Bhima were sent, one after the other, on a similar quest; but neither returned, having drunk of the lake and dropped down dead. Then Yudhishthira rose up to go in search of his brothers. At length, he came to the beautiful lake and saw his brothers lying dead. His heart was full of grief at the sight, and he began to lament. Suddenly he heard the same voice saying, "Do not, O child, act rashly. I am a Yaksha living as a crane on tiny fish. It is by me that thy younger brothers have been brought under the sway of the Lord of departed spirits. If thou, O Prince, answer not the questions put by me even thou shalt number the fifth corpse. Having answered my questions first, do thou, O Kunti's son, drink and carry away as much as thou requires"." Yudhishthira replied, "I shall answer thy questions according to my intelligence. Do thou ask met" The Yaksha then asked him several questions, all of which Yudhishthira answered satisfactorily. One of the questions asked was: "What is the most wonderful fact in this world?" "We see our fellow-beings every moment falling off around us; but those that are left behind think that they will never die. This is the most curious fact: in face of death, none believes that he will die! " Another question asked was: "What is the path of knowing the secret of religion?" And Yudhishthira answered, "By argument nothing can be settled; doctrines there are many; various are the scriptures, one part contradicting the other. There are not two sages who do not differ in their opinions. The secret of religion is buried deep, as it were, in dark caves. So the path to be followed is that which the great ones have trodden." Then the Yaksha said, "I am pleased. I am Dharma, he God of Justice in the form of the crane. I came to test you. Now, your brothers, see, not one of them is dead. It is all my magic. Since abstention from injury is regarded by thee as higher than both profit and pleasure, therefore, let all thy brothers live, O Bull of the Bharata race." And at these words of the Yaksha, the Pandavas rose up.

Here is a glimpse of the nature of King Yudhishthira. We find by his answers that he was more of a philosopher, more of a Yogi, than a king.

Now, as the thirteenth year of the exile was drawing nigh, the Yaksha bade them go to Virâta's kingdom and live there in such disguises as they would think best.

So, after the term of the twelve years' exile had expired, they went to the kingdom of Virata in different disguises to spend the remaining one year in concealment, and entered into menial service in the king's household. Thus Yudhishthira became a Brâhmana courtier of the king, as one skilled in dice; Bhima was appointed a cook; Arjuna, dressed as a eunuch, was made a teacher of dancing and music to Uttarâ, the princess, and remained in the inner apartments of the king; Nakula became the keeper of the king's horses; and Sahadeva got the charge of the cows; and Draupadi, disguised as a waiting-woman, was also admitted into the queen's household. Thus concealing their identity the Pandava brothers safely spent a year, and the search of Duryodhana to find them out was of no avail. They were only discovered just when the year was out.

Then Yudhishthira sent an ambassador to Dhritarashtra and demanded that half of the kingdom should, as their share, be restored to them. But Duryodhana hated his cousins and would not consent to their legitimate demands. They were even willing to accept a single province, nay, even five villages. But the headstrong Duryodhana declared that he would not yield without fight even as much land as a needle's point would hold. Dhritarashtra pleaded again and again for peace, but all in vain. Krishna also went and tried to avert the impending war and death of kinsmen, so did the wise elders of the royal court; but all negotiations for a peaceful partition of the kingdom were futile. So, at last, preparations were made on both sides for war, and all the warlike nations took part in it.

The old Indian customs of the Kshatriyas were observed in it. Duryodhana took one side, Yudhishthira the other. From Yudhishthira messengers were at once sent to all the surrounding kings, entreating their alliance, since honourable men would grant the request that first reached them. So, warriors from all parts assembled to espouse the cause of either the Pandavas or the Kurus according to the precedence of their requests; and thus one brother joined this side, and the other that side, the father on one side, and the son on the other. The most curious thing was the code of war of those days; as soon as the battle for the day ceased and evening came, the opposing parties were good friends, even going to each other's tents; however, when the morning came, again they proceeded to fight each other. That was the strange trait that the Hindus carried down to the time of the Mohammedan invasion. Then again, a man on horseback must not strike one on foot; must not poison the weapon; must not vanquish the enemy in any unequal fight, or by dishonesty; and must never take undue advantage of another, and so on. If any deviated from these rules he would be covered with dishonour and shunned. The Kshatriyas were trained in that way. And when the foreign invasion came from Central Asia, the Hindus treated the invaders in the selfsame way. They defeated them several times, and on as many occasions sent them back to their homes with presents etc. The code laid down was that they must not usurp anybody's country; and when a man was beaten, he must be sent back to his country with due regard to his position. The Mohammedan conquerors treated the Hindu kings differently, and when they got them once, they destroyed them without remorse.

Mind you, in those days — in the times of our story, the poem says — the science of arms was not the mere use of bows and arrows at all; it was magic archery in which the use of Mantras, concentration, etc., played a prominent part. One man could fight millions of men and burn them at will. He could send one arrow, and it would rain thousands of arrows and thunder; he could make anything burn, and so on — it was all divine magic. One fact is most curious in both these poems — the Ramayana and the Mahabharata — along with these magic arrows and all these things going on, you see the cannon already in use. The cannon is an old, old thing, used by the Chinese and the Hindus. Upon the walls of the cities were hundreds of curious weapons made of hollow iron tubes, which filled with powder and ball would kill hundreds of men. The people believed that the Chinese, by magic, put the devil inside a hollow iron tube, and when they applied a little fire to a hole, the devil came out with a terrific noise and killed many people.

So in those old days, they used to fight with magic arrows. One man would be able to fight millions of others. They had their military arrangements and tactics: there were the foot soldiers, termed the Pâda; then the cavalry, Turaga; and two other divisions which the moderns have lost and given up — there was the elephant corps — hundreds and hundreds of elephants, with men on their backs, formed into regiments and protected with huge sheets of iron mail; and these elephants would bear down upon a mass of the enemy — then, there were the chariots, of course (you have all seen pictures of those old chariots, they were used in every country). These were the four divisions of the army in those old days.

Now, both parties alike wished to secure the alliance of Krishna. But he declined to take an active part and fight in this war, but offered himself as charioteer to Arjuna, and as the friend and counsellor of the Pandavas while to Duryodhana he gave his army of mighty soldiers.

Then was fought on the vast plain of Kurukshetra the great battle in which Bhisma, Drona, Karna, and the brothers of Duryodhana with the kinsmen on both sides and thousands of other heroes fell. The war lasted eighteen days. Indeed, out of the eighteen Akshauhinis of soldiers very few men were left. The death of Duryodhana ended the war in favour of the Pandavas. It was followed by the lament of Gândhâri, the queen and the widowed women, and the funerals of the deceased warriors.

The greatest incident of the war was the marvellous and immortal poem of the Gitâ, the Song Celestial. It is the popular scripture of India and the loftiest of all teachings. It consists of a dialogue held by Arjuna with Krishna, just before the commencement of the fight on the battle-field of Kurukshetra. I would advise those of you who have not read that book to read it. If you only knew how much it has influenced your own country even! If you want to know the source of Emerson's inspiration, it is this book, the Gita. He went to see Carlyle, and Carlyle made him a present of the Gita; and that little book is responsible for the Concord Movement. All the broad movements in America, in one way or other, are indebted to the Concord party.

The central figure of the Gita is Krishna. As you worship Jesus of Nazareth as God come down as man so the Hindus worship many Incarnations of God. They believe in not one or two only, but in many, who have come down from time to time, according to the needs of the world, for the preservation of Dharma and destruction of wickedness. Each sect has one, and Krishna is one of them. Krishna, perhaps, has a larger number of followers in India than any other Incarnation of God. His followers hold that he was the most perfect of those Incarnations. Why? "Because," they say, "look at Buddha and other Incarnations: they were only monks, and they had no sympathy for married people. How could they have? But look at Krishna: he was great as a son, as a king, as a father, and all through his life he practiced the marvellous teachings which he preached." "He who in the midst of the greatest activity finds the sweetest peace, and in the midst of the greatest calmness is most active, he has known the secret of life." Krishna shows the way how to do this — by being non-attached: do everything but do not get identified with anything. You are the soul, the pure, the free, all the time; you are the Witness. Our misery comes, not from work, but by our getting attached to something. Take for instance, money: money is a great thing to have, earn it, says Krishna; struggle hard to get money, but don't get attached to it. So with children, with wife, husband, relatives, fame, everything; you have no need to shun them, only don't get attached. There is only one attachment and that belongs to the Lord, and to none other. Work for them, love them, do good to them, sacrifice a hundred lives, if need be, for them, but never be attached. His own life was the exact exemplification of that.

Remember that the book which delineates the life of Krishna is several thousand years old, and some parts of his life are very similar to those of Jesus of Nazareth. Krishna was of royal birth; there was a tyrant king, called Kamsa, and there was a prophecy that one would be born of such and such a family, who would be king. So Kamsa ordered all the male children to be massacred. The father and mother of Krishna were cast by King Kamsa into prison, where the child was born. A light suddenly shone in the prison and the child spoke saying, "I am the Light of the world, born for the good of the world." You find Krishna again symbolically represented with cows — "The Great Cowherd," as he is called. Sages affirmed that God Himself was born, and they went to pay him homage. In other parts of the story, the similarity between the two does not continue.

Shri Krishna conquered this tyrant Kamsa, but he never thought of accepting or occupying the throne himself. He had nothing to do with that. He had done his duty and there it ended.

After the conclusion of the Kurukshetra War, the great warrior and venerable grandsire, Bhishma, who fought ten days out of the eighteen days' battle, still lay on his deathbed and gave instructions to Yudhishthira on various subjects, such as the duties of the king, the duties of the four castes, the four stages of life, the laws of marriage, the bestowing of gifts, etc., basing them on the teachings of the ancient sages. He explained Sânkhya philosophy and Yoga philosophy and narrated numerous tales and traditions about saints and gods and kings. These teachings occupy nearly one-fourth of the entire work and form an invaluable storehouse of Hindu laws and moral codes. Yudhishthira had in the meantime been crowned king. But the awful bloodshed and extinction of superiors and relatives weighed heavily on his mind; and then, under the advice of Vyasa, he performed the Ashvamedha sacrifice.

After the war, for fifteen years Dhritarashtra dwelt in peace and honour, obeyed by Yudhishthira and his brothers. Then the aged monarch leaving Yudhishthira on the throne, retired to the forest with his devoted wife and Kunti, the mother of the Pandava brothers, to pass his last days in asceticism.

Thirty-six years had now passed since Yudhishthira regained his empire. Then came to him the news that Krishna had left his mortal body. Krishna, the sage, his friend, his prophet, his counsellor, had departed. Arjuna hastened to Dwârâka and came back only to confirm the sad news that Krishna and the Yâdavas were all dead. Then the king and the other brothers, overcome with sorrow, declared that the time for them to go, too, had arrived. So they cast off the burden of royalty, placed Parikshit, the grandson of Arjuna, on the throne, and retired to the Himalayas, on the Great Journey, the Mahâprasthâna. This was a peculiar form of Sannyâsa. It was a custom for old kings to become Sannyasins. In ancient India, when men became very old, they would give up everything. So did the kings. When a man did not want to live any more, then he went towards the Himalayas, without eating or drinking and walked on and on till the body failed. All the time thinking of God, be just marched on till the body gave way.

Then came the gods, the sages, and they told King Yudhishthira that he should go and reach heaven. To go to heaven one has to cross the highest peaks of the Himalayas. Beyond the Himalayas is Mount Meru. On the top of Mount Meru is heaven. None ever went there in this body. There the gods reside. And Yudhishthira was called upon by the gods to go there.

So the five brothers and their wife clad themselves in robes of bark, and set out on their journey. On the way, they were followed by a dog. On and on they went, and they turned their weary feet northward to where the Himalayas lifts his lofty peaks, and they saw the mighty Mount Meru in front of them. Silently they walked on in the snow, until suddenly the queen fell, to rise no more. To Yudhishthira who was leading the way, Bhima, one of the brothers, said, "Behold, O King, the queen has fallen." The king shed tears, but he did not look back. "We are going to meet Krishna," he says. "No time to look back. March on." After a while, again Bhima said, "Behold, our brother, Sahadeva has fallen." The king shed tears; but paused not. "March on," he cried.

One after the other, in the cold and snow, all the four brothers dropped down, but unshaken, though alone, the king advanced onward. Looking behind, he saw the faithful dog was still following him. And so the king and the dog went on, through snow and ice, over hill and dale, climbing higher and higher, till they reached Mount Meru; and there they began to hear the chimes of heaven, and celestial flowers were showered upon the virtuous king by the gods. Then descended the chariot of the gods, and Indra prayed him, "Ascend in this chariot, greatest of mortals: thou that alone art given to enter heaven without changing the mortal body." But no, that Yudhishthira would not do without his devoted brothers and his queen; then Indra explained to him that the brothers had already gone thither before him.

And Yudhishthira looked around and said to his dog, "Get into the chariot, child." The god stood aghast. "What! the dog?" he cried. "Do thou cast off this dog! The dog goeth not to heaven! Great King, what dost thou mean? Art thou mad? Thou, the most virtuous of the human race, thou only canst go to heaven in thy body." "But he has been my devoted companion through snow and ice. When all my brothers were dead, my queen dead, he alone never left me. How can I leave him now?" "There is no place in heaven for men with dogs. He has to be left behind. There is nothing unrighteous in this." "I do not go to heaven," replied the king, "without the dog. I shall never give up such a one who has taken refuge with me, until my own life is at an end. I shall never swerve from righteousness, nay, not even for the joys of heaven or the urging of a god." "Then," said Indra, "on one condition the dog goes to heaven. You have been the most virtuous of mortals and he has been a dog, killing and eating animals; he is sinful, hunting, and taking other lives. You can exchange heaven with him. "Agreed," says the king. "Let the dog go to heaven."

At once, the scene changed. Hearing these noble words of Yudhishthira, the dog revealed himself as Dharma; the dog was no other than Yama, the Lord of Death and Justice. And Dharma exclaimed, "Behold, O King, no man was ever so unselfish as thou, willing to exchange heaven with a little dog, and for his sake disclaiming all his virtues and ready to go to hell even for him. Thou art well born, O King of kings. Thou hast compassion for all creatures, O Bhârata, of which this is a bright example. Hence, regions of undying felicity are thine! Thou hast won them, O King, and shine is a celestial and high goal."

Then Yudhishthira, with Indra, Dharma, and other gods, proceeds to heaven in a celestial car. He undergoes some trials, bathes in the celestial Ganga, and assumes a celestial body. He meets his brothers who are now immortals, and all at last is bliss.

Thus ends the story of the Mahabharata, setting forth in a sublime poem the triumph of virtue and defeat of vice.

In speaking of the Mahabharata to you, it is simply impossible for me to present the unending array of the grand and majestic characters of the mighty heroes depicted by the genius and master-mind of Vyasa. The internal conflicts between righteousness and filial affection in the mind of the god-fearing, yet feeble, old, blind King Dhritarashtra; the majestic character of the grandsire Bhishma; the noble and virtuous nature of the royal Yudhishthira, and of the other four brothers, as mighty in valour as in devotion and loyalty; the peerless character of Krishna, unsurpassed in human wisdom; and not less brilliant, the characters of the women — the stately queen Gandhari, the loving mother Kunti, the ever-devoted and all-suffering Draupadi — these and hundreds of other characters of this Epic and those of the Ramayana have been the cherished heritage of the whole Hindu world for the last several thousands of years and form the basis of their thoughts and of their moral and ethical ideas. In fact, the Ramayana and the Mahabharata are the two encyclopaedias of the ancient Aryan life and wisdom, portraying an ideal civilisation which humanity has yet to aspire after.

Thoughts On The Gita

During his sojourn in Calcutta in 1897, Swami Vivekananda used to stay for the most part at the Math, the headquarters of the Ramakrisnna Mission, located then at Alambazar. During this time several young men, who had been preparing themselves for some time previously, gathered round him and took the vows of Brahmacharya and Sannyâsa, and Swamiji began to train them for future work, by holding classes on the Gitâ and Vedanta, and initiating them into the practices of meditation. In one of these classes he talked eloquently in Bengali on the Gita. The following is the translation of the summary of the discourse as it was entered in the Math diary:

The book known as the Gita forms a part of the Mahâbhârata. To understand the Gita properly, several things are very important to know. First, whether it formed a part of the Mahabharata, i.e. whether the authorship attributed to Veda-Vyâsa was true, or if it was merely interpolated within the great epic; secondly, whether there was any historical personality of the name of Krishna; thirdly, whether the great war of Kurukshetra as mentioned in the Gita actually took place; and fourthly, whether Arjuna and others were real historical persons.

Now in the first place, let us see what grounds there are for such inquiry. We know that there were many who went by the name of Veda-Vyasa; and among them who was the real author of the Gita — the Bâdarâyana Vyasa or Dvaipâyana Vyasa? "Vyasa" was only a title. Anyone who composed a new Purâna was known by the name of Vyasa, like the word Vikramâditya, which was also a general name. Another point is, the book, Gita, had not been much known to the generality of people before Shankarâchârya made it famous by writing his great commentary on it. Long before that, there was current, according to many, the commentary on it by Bodhâyana. If this could be proved, it would go a long way, no doubt, to establish the antiquity of the Gita and the authorship of Vyasa. But the Bodhayana Bhâshya on the *Vedânta Sutras* — from which Râmânuja compiled his *Shri-Bhâshya*, which Shankaracharya mentions and even quotes in part here and there in his own commentary, and which was so greatly discussed by the Swami Dayânanda — not a copy even of that Bodhayana Bhashya could I find while travelling throughout India. It is said that even Ramanuja compiled his Bhashya from a worm-eaten manuscript which he happened to find. When even this great Bodhayana Bhashya on the *Vedanta-Sutras* is so much enshrouded in the darkness of uncertainty, it is simply useless to try to establish the existence of the Bodhayana Bhashya on the Gita. Some infer that Shankaracharya was the author of the Gita, and that it was he who foisted it into the body of the Mahabharata.

Then as to the second point in question, much doubt exists about the personality of Krishna. In one place in the Chhândogya Upanishad we find mention of Krishna, the son of Devaki, who received spiritual instructions from one Ghora, a Yogi. In the Mahabharata, Krishna is the king of Dwârakâ; and in the *Vishnu Purâna* we find a description of Krishna playing with the Gopis. Again, in the *Bhâgavata*, the account of his Râsalilâ is detailed at length. In very ancient times in our country there was in vogue an Utsava called Madanotsava (celebration in honour of Cupid). That very thing was transformed into Dola and thrust upon the shoulders of Krishna. Who can be so bold as to assert that the Rasalila and other things connected with him were not similarly fastened upon him? In ancient times there was very little tendency in our country to find out truths by historical research. So any one could say what he thought best without substantiating it with proper facts and evidence. Another thing: in those ancient times there was very little hankering after name and fame in men. So it often happened that one man composed a book and made it pass current in the name of his Guru or of someone else. In such cases it is very hazardous for the investigator of historical facts to get at the truth. In ancient times they had no knowledge whatever of geography; imagination ran riot. And so we meet with such fantastic creations of the brain as sweet-ocean, milk-ocean, clarified-butter-ocean, curd-ocean, etc! In the Puranas, we find one living ten thousand years, another a hundred thousand years! But the Vedas say, शतायुर्वै पुरुषः "Man lives a hundred years." Whom shall we follow here? So, to reach a correct conclusion in the case of Krishna is well-nigh impossible.

It is human nature to build round the real character of a great man all sorts of imaginary superhuman attributes. As regards Krishna the same must have happened, but it seems quite probable that he was a king. Quite probable I say, because in ancient times in our country it was chiefly the kings who exerted themselves most in the preaching of Brahma-Jnâna. Another point to be especially noted here is that whoever might have been the author of the Gita, we find its teachings the same as those in the whole of the Mahabharata. From this we can safely infer that in the age of the Mahabharata some great man arose and preached the Brahma-Jnâna in this new garb to the then existing society. Another fact comes to the fore that in the olden days, as one sect after another arose, there also came into existence and use among them one new scripture or another. It happened, too, that in the lapse of time both the sect and its scripture died out, or the sect ceased to exist but its scripture remained. Similarly, it was quite probable that the Gita was the scripture of such a sect which had embodied its high and noble ideas in this sacred book.

Now to the third point, bearing on the subject of the Kurukshetra War, no special evidence in support of it can be adduced. But there is no doubt that there was a war fought between the Kurus and the Panchâlas. Another thing: how could there be so much discussion about Jnâna, Bhakti, and Yoga on the battle-field, where the huge army stood in battle array ready to fight, just waiting for the last signal? And was any shorthand writer present there to note down every word spoken between Krishna and Arjuna, in the din and turmoil of the battle-field? According to some, this Kurukshetra War is only an allegory. When we sum up its esoteric significance, it means the war which is constantly going on within man between the tendencies of good and evil. This meaning, too, may not be irrational.

About the fourth point, there is enough ground of doubt as regards the historicity of Arjuna and others, and it is this: Shatapatha Brâhmana is a very ancient book. In it are mentioned somewhere all the names of those who were the performers of the Ashvamedha Yajna: but in those places there is not only no mention, but no hint even of the names of Arjuna and others, though it speaks of Janamejaya, the son of Parikshit who was a grandson of Arjuna. Yet in the Mahabharata and other books it is stated that Yudhishthira, Arjuna, and others celebrated the Ashvamedha sacrifice.

One thing should be especially remembered here, that there is no connection between these historical researches and our real aim, which is the knowledge that leads to the acquirement of Dharma. Even if the historicity of the whole thing is proved to be absolutely false today, it will not in the least be any loss to us. Then what is the use of so much historical research, you may ask. It has its use, because we have to get at the truth; it will not do for us to remain bound by wrong ideas born of ignorance. In this country people think very little of the importance of such inquiries. Many of the sects believe that in order to preach a good thing which may be beneficial to many, there is no harm in telling an untruth, if that helps such preaching, or in other words, the end justifies the means. Hence we find many of our Tantras beginning with, "Mahâdeva said to Pârvati". But our duty should be to convince ourselves of the truth, to believe in truth only. Such is the power of superstition, or faith in old traditions without inquiry into its truth, that it keeps men bound hand and foot, so much so, that even Jesus the Christ, Mohammed, and other great men believed in many such superstitions and could not shake them off. You have to keep your eye always fixed on truth only and shun all superstitions completely.

Now it is for us to see what there is in the Gita. If we study the Upanishads we notice, in wandering through the mazes of many irrelevant subjects, the sudden introduction of the discussion of a great truth, just as in the midst of a huge wilderness a traveller unexpectedly comes across here and there an exquisitely beautiful rose, with its leaves, thorns, roots, all entangled. Compared with that, the Gita is like these truths beautifully arranged together in their proper places — like a fine garland or a bouquet of the choicest flowers. The Upanishads deal elaborately with Shraddhâ in many places, but hardly mention Bhakti. In the Gita, on the other hand, the subject of Bhakti is not only again and again dealt with, but in it, the innate spirit of Bhakti has attained its culmination.

Now let us see some of the main points discussed in the Gita. Wherein lies the originality of the Gita which distinguishes it from all preceding scriptures? It is this: Though before its advent, Yoga, Jnana, Bhakti, etc. had each its strong adherents, they all quarrelled among themselves, each claiming superiority for his own chosen path; no one ever tried to seek for reconciliation among these different paths. It was the author of the Gita who for the first time tried to harmonise these. He took the best from what all the sects then existing had to offer and threaded them in the Gita. But even where Krishna failed to show a complete reconciliation (Samanvaya) among these warring sects, it was fully accomplished by Ramakrishna Paramahamsa in this nineteenth century.

The next is, Nishkâma Karma, or work without desire or attachment. People nowadays understand what is meant by this in various ways. Some say what is implied by being unattached is to become purposeless. If that were its real meaning, then heartless brutes and the walls would be the best exponents of the performance of Nishkama Karma. Many others, again, give the example of Janaka, and wish themselves to be equally recognised as past masters in the practice of Nishkama Karma! Janaka (lit. father) did not acquire that distinction by bringing forth children, but these people all want to be Janakas, with the sole qualification of being the fathers of a brood of children! No! The true Nishkama Karmi (performer of work without desire) is neither to be like a brute, nor to be inert, nor heartless. He is not Tâmasika but of pure Sattva. His heart is so full of love and sympathy that he can embrace the whole world with his love. The world at large cannot generally comprehend his all-embracing love and sympathy.

The reconciliation of the different paths of Dharma, and work without desire or attachment — these are the two special characteristics of the Gita.

Let us now read a little from the second chapter.

सञ्जय उवाच ॥

तं तथा कृपयाविष्टमश्रुपूर्णाकुलेक्षणम् ।
विषीदन्तमिदं वाक्यमुवाच मधुसूदन: ॥१॥

श्रीभगवानुवाच ॥

कुतस्त्वा कश्मलमिदं विषमे समुपस्थितम् ।
अनार्यजुष्टमस्वर्ग्यमकीर्तिकरमर्जुन ॥२॥

क्लैब्यं मा स्म गम: पार्थ नैतत्त्वय्युपपद्यते ।
क्षुद्रं हृदयदौर्बल्यं त्यक्त्वोत्तिष्ठ परंतप ॥३॥

"Sanjaya said:

To him who was thus overwhelmed with pity and sorrowing, and whose eyes were dimmed with tears, Madhusudana spoke these words.

The Blessed Lord said:

In such a strait, whence comes upon thee, O Arjuna, this dejection, un-Aryan-like, disgraceful, and contrary to the attainment of heaven?

Yield not to unmanliness, O son of Prithâ! Ill doth it become thee. Cast off this mean faint-heartedness and arise, O scorcher of thine enemies!"

In the Shlokas beginning with , how poetically, how beautifully, has Arjuna's real position been painted! Then Shri Krishna advises Arjuna; and in the words etc., why is he goading Arjuna to fight? Because it was not that the disinclination of Arjuna to fight arose out of the overwhelming predominance of pure Sattva Guna; it was all Tamas that brought on this unwillingness. The nature of a man of Sattva Guna is, that he is equally calm in all situations in life — whether it be prosperity or adversity. But Arjuna was afraid, he was overwhelmed with pity. That he had the instinct and the inclination to fight is proved by the simple fact that he came to the battle-field with no other purpose than that. Frequently in our lives also such things are seen to happen. Many people think they are Sâttvika by nature, but they are really nothing but Tâmasika. Many living in an uncleanly way regard themselves as Paramahamsas! Why? Because the Shâstras say that Paramahamsas live like one inert, or mad, or like an unclean spirit. Paramahamsas are compared to children, but here it should be understood that the comparison is one-sided. The Paramahamsa and the child are not one and non-different. They only appear similar, being the two extreme poles, as it were. One has reached to a state beyond Jnana, and the other has not got even an inkling of Jnana. The quickest and the gentlest vibrations of light are both beyond the reach of our ordinary vision; but in the one it is intense heat, and in the other it may be said to be almost without any heat. So it is with the opposite qualities of Sattva and Tamas. They seem in some respects to be the same, no doubt, but there is a world of difference between them. The Tamoguna loves very much to array itself in the garb of the Sattva. Here, in Arjuna, the mighty warrior, it has come under the guise of Dayâ (pity).

In order to remove this delusion which had overtaken Arjuna, what did the Bhagavân say? As I always preach that you should not decry a man by calling him a sinner, but that you should draw his attention to the omnipotent power that is in him, in the same way does the Bhagavan speak to Arjuna. नैतत्त्वय्युपपद्यते — "It doth not befit thee!" "Thou art Atman imperishable, beyond all evil. Having forgotten thy real nature, thou hast, by thinking thyself a sinner, as one afflicted with bodily evils and mental grief, thou hast made thyself so — this doth not befit thee!" — so says the Bhagavan: क्लैब्यं मा स्म गम: पार्थ — Yield not to unmanliness, O son of Pritha. There is in the world neither sin nor misery, neither disease nor grief; if there is anything in the world which can be called sin, it is this — 'fear'; know that any work which brings out the latent power in thee is Punya (virtue); and that which makes thy body and mind weak is, verily, sin. Shake off this weakness, this faintheartedness! क्लैब्यं मा स्म गम: पार्थ । — Thou art a hero, a Vira; this is unbecoming of thee."

If you, my sons, can proclaim this message to the world — क्लैब्यं मा स्म गम: पार्थ नैतत्त्वय्युपपद्यते — then all this disease, grief, sin, and sorrow will vanish from off the face of the earth in three days. All these ideas of weakness will be nowhere. Now it is everywhere — this current of the vibration of fear. Reverse the current: bring in the opposite vibration, and behold the magic transformation! Thou art omnipotent — go, go to the mouth of the cannon, fear not.

Hate not the most abject sinner, fool; not to his exterior. Turn thy gaze inward, where resides the Paramâtman. Proclaim to the whole world with trumpet voice, "There is no sin in thee, there is no misery in thee; thou art the reservoir of omnipotent power. Arise, awake, and manifest the Divinity within!"

If one reads this one Shloka —

क्लैब्यं मा स्म गम: पार्थ नैतत्त्वय्युपपद्यते ।
क्षुद्रं हृदयदौर्बल्यं त्यक्त्वोत्तिष्ठ परंतप ॥

— one gets all the merits of reading the entire Gita; for in this one Shloka lies imbedded the whole Message of the Gita.

The Story Of Jada Bharata

(Delivered in California)

There was a great monarch named Bharata. The land which is called India by foreigners is known to her children as Bhârata Varsha. Now, it is enjoined on every Hindu when he becomes old, to give up all worldly pursuits — to leave the cares of the world, its wealth, happiness, and enjoyments to his son — and retire into the forest, there to meditate upon the Self which is the only reality in him, and thus break the bonds which bind him to life. King or priest, peasant or servant, man or woman, none is exempt from this duty: for all the duties of the householder — of the son, the brother, the husband, the father, the wife, the daughter, the mother, the sister — are but preparations towards that one stage, when all the bonds which bind the soul to matter are severed asunder for ever.

The great king Bharata in his old age gave over his throne to his son, and retired into the forest. He who had been ruler over millions and millions of subjects, who had lived in marble palaces, inlaid with gold and silver, who had drunk out of jewelled cups — this king built a little cottage with his own hands, made of reeds and grass, on the banks of a river in the Himalayan forests. There he lived on roots and wild herbs, collected by his own hands, and constantly meditated upon Him who is always present in the soul of man. Days, months, and years passed. One day, a deer came to drink water near by where the royal sage was meditating. At the same moment, a lion roared at a little distance off. The deer was so terrified that she, without satisfying her thirst, made a big jump to cross the river. The deer was with young, and this extreme exertion and sudden fright made her give birth to a little fawn, and immediately after she fell dead. The fawn fell into the water and was being carried rapidly away by the foaming stream, when it caught the eyes of the king. The king rose from his position of meditation and rescuing the fawn from the water, took it to his cottage, made a fire, and with care and attention fondled the little thing back to life. Then the kindly sage took the fawn under his protection, bringing it up on soft grass and fruits. The fawn thrived under the paternal care of the retired monarch, and grew into a beautiful deer. Then, he whose mind had been strong enough to break away from lifelong attachment to power, position, and family, became attached to the deer which he had saved from the stream. And as he became fonder and fonder of the deer, the less and less he could concentrate his mind upon the Lord. When the deer went out to graze in the forest, if it were late in returning, the mind of the royal sage would become anxious and worried. He would think, "Perhaps my little one has been attacked by some tiger — or perhaps some other danger has befallen it; otherwise, why is it late?"

Some years passed in this way, but one day death came, and the royal sage laid himself down to die. But his mind, instead of being intent upon the Self, was thinking about the deer; and with his eyes fixed upon the sad looks of his beloved deer, his soul left the body. As the result of this, in the next birth he was born as a deer. But no Karma is lost, and all the great and good deeds done by him as a king and sage bore their fruit. This deer was a born Jâtismara, and remembered his past birth, though he was bereft of speech and was living in an animal body. He always left his companions and was instinctively drawn to graze near hermitages where oblations were offered and the Upanishads were preached.

After the usual years of a deer's life had been spent, it died and was next born as the youngest son of a rich Brahmin. And in that life also, he remembered all his past, and even in his childhood was determined no more to get entangled in the good and evil of life. The child, as it grew up, was strong and healthy, but would not speak a word, and lived as one inert and insane, for fear of getting mixed up with worldly affairs. His thoughts were always on the Infinite, and he lived only to wear out his past Prârabdha Karma. In course of time the father died, and the sons divided the property among themselves; and thinking that the youngest was a dumb, good-for-nothing man, they seized his share. Their charity, however, extended only so far as to give him enough food to live upon. The wives of the brothers were often very harsh to him, putting him to do all the hard work; and if he was unable to do everything they wanted, they would treat him very unkindly. But he showed neither vexation nor fear, and neither did he speak a word. When they persecuted him very much, he would stroll out of the house and sit under a tree, by the hour, until their wrath was appeased, and then he would quietly go home again.

One day; when the wives of the brothers had treated him with more than usual unkindness, Bharata went out of the house, seated himself under the shadow of a tree and rested. Now it happened that the king of the country was passing by, carried in a palanquin on the shoulders of bearers. One of the bearers had unexpectedly fallen ill, and so his attendants were looking about for a man to replace him. They came upon Bharata seated under a tree; and seeing he was a strong young man, they asked him if he would take the place of the sick man in bearing the king's palanquin. But Bharata did not reply. Seeing that he was so able-bodied, the king's servants caught hold of him and placed the pole on his shoulders. Without speaking a word, Bharata went on. Very soon after this, the king remarked that the palanquin was not being evenly carried, and looking out of the palanquin addressed the new bearer, saying "Fool, rest a while; if thy shoulders pain thee, rest a while." Then Bharata laying the pole of the palanquin down, opened his lips for the first time in his life, and spoke, "Whom dost thou, O King, call a fool? Whom dost thou ask to lay down the palanquin? Who dost thou say is weary? Whom dost thou address as 'thou'? If thou meanest, O King, by the word 'thee' this mass of flesh, it is composed of the same matter as thine; it is unconscious, and it knoweth no weariness, it knoweth no pain. If it is the mind, the mind is the same as thine; it is universal. But if the word 'thee' is applied to something beyond that, then it is the Self, the Reality in me, which is the same as in thee, and it is the One in the universe. Dost thou mean, O King, that the Self can ever be weary, that It can ever be tired, that It can ever be hurt? I did not want, O King — this body did not want — to trample upon the poor worms crawling on the road, and therefore, in trying to avoid them, the palanquin moved unevenly. But the Self was never tired; It was never weak; It never bore the pole of the palanquin: for It is omnipotent and omnipresent." And so he dwelt eloquently on the nature of the soul, and on the highest knowledge, etc. The king, who was proud of his learning, knowledge, and philosophy, alighted from the palanquin, and fell at the feet of Bharata, saying, "I ask thy pardon, O mighty one, I did not know that thou wast a sage, when I asked thee to carry me." Bharata blessed him and departed. He then resumed the even tenor of his previous life. When Bharata left the body, he was freed for ever from the bondage of birth.

The Story Of Prahlada

(Delivered in California)

Hiranyakashipu was the king of the Daityas. The Daityas, though born of the same parentage as the Devas or gods, were always, at war with the latter. The Daityas had no part in the oblations and offerings of mankind, or in the government of the world and its guidance. But sometimes they waxed strong and drove all the Devas from the heaven, and seized the throne of the gods and ruled for a time. Then the Devas prayed to Vishnu, the Omnipresent Lord of the universe, and He helped them out of their difficulty. The Daityas were driven out, and once more the gods reigned. Hiranyakashipu, king of the Daityas, in his turn, succeeded in conquering his cousins, the Devas, and seated himself on the throne of the heavens and ruled the three worlds — the middle world, inhabited by men and animals; the heavens, inhabited by gods and godlike beings; and the nether world, inhabited by the Daityas. Now, Hiranyakashipu declared himself to be the God of the whole universe and proclaimed that there was no other God but himself, and strictly enjoined that the Omnipotent Vishnu should have no worship offered to Him anywhere; and that all the worship should henceforth be given to himself only.

Hiranyakashipu had a son called Prahlâda. Now, it so happened, that this Prahlada from his infancy was devoted to God. He showed indications of this as a child; and the king of the Daityas, fearing that the evil he wanted to drive away from the world would crop up in his own family, made over his son to two teachers called Shanda and Amarka, who were very stern disciplinarians, with strict injunctions that Prahlada was never to hear even the name of Vishnu mentioned. The teachers took the prince to their home, and there he was put to study with the other children of his age. But the little Prahlada, instead of learning from his books, devoted all the time in teaching the other boys how to worship Vishnu. When the teachers found it out, they were frightened, for the fear of the mighty king Hiranyakashipu was upon them, and they tried their best to dissuade the child from such teachings. But Prahlada could no more stop his teaching and worshipping Vishnu than he could stop breathing. To clear themselves, the teachers told the terrible fact to the king, that his son was not only worshipping Vishnu himself, but also spoiling all the other children by teaching them to worship Vishnu.

The monarch became very much enraged when he heard this and called the boy to his presence. He tried by gentle persuasions to dissuade Prahlada from the worship of Vishnu and taught him that he, the king, was the only God to worship. But it was to no purpose. The child declared, again and again, that the Omnipresent Vishnu, Lord of the universe, was the only Being to be worshipped — for even he, the king, held his throne only so long as it pleased Vishnu. The rage of the king knew no bounds, and he ordered the boy to be immediately killed. So the Daityas struck him with pointed weapons; but Prahlad's mind was so intent upon Vishnu that he felt no pain from them.

When his father, the king, saw that it was so, he became frightened but, roused to the worst passions of a Daitya, contrived various diabolical means to kill the boy. He ordered him to be trampled under foot by an elephant. The enraged elephant could not crush the body any more than he could have crushed a block of iron. So this measure also was to no purpose. Then the king ordered the boy to be thrown over a precipice, and this order too was duly carried out; but, as Vishnu resided in the heart of Prahlada, he came down upon the earth as gently as a flower drops upon the grass. Poison, fire, starvation, throwing into a well, enchantments, and other measures were then tried on the child one after another, but to no purpose. Nothing could hurt him in whose heart dwelt Vishnu.

At last, the king ordered the boy to be tied with mighty serpents called up from the nether worlds, and then cast to the bottom of the ocean, where huge mountains were to be piled high upon him, so that in course of time, if not immediately, he might die; and he ordered him to be left in this plight. Even though treated in this manner, the boy continued to pray to his beloved Vishnu: "Salutation to Thee, Lord of the universe. Thou beautiful Vishnu!" Thus thinking and meditating on Vishnu, he began to feel that Vishnu was near him, nay, that He was in his own soul, until he began to feel that he was Vishnu, and that he was everything and everywhere.

As soon as he realised this, all the snake bonds snapped asunder; the mountains were pulverised, the ocean upheaved, and he was gently lifted up above the waves, and safely carried to the shore. As Prahlada stood there, he forgot that he was a Daitya and had a mortal body: he felt he was

the universe and all the powers of the universe emanated from him; there
was nothing in nature that could injure him; he himself was the ruler of
nature. Time passed thus, in one unbroken ecstasy of bliss, until gradually
Prahlada began to remember that he had a body and that he was Prahlada.
As soon as he became once more conscious of the body, he saw that God
was within and without; and everything appeared to him as Vishnu.

When the king Hiranyakashipu found to his horror that all mortal
means of getting rid of the boy who was perfectly devoted to his enemy, the
God Vishnu, were powerless, he was at a loss to know what to do. The king
had the boy again brought before him, and tried to persuade him once more
to listen to his advice, through gentle means. But Prahlada made the same
reply. Thinking, however, that these childish whims of the boy would be
rectified with age and further training, he put him again under the charge
of the teachers, Shanda and Amarka, asking them to teach him the duties
of the king. But those teachings did not appeal to Prahlada, and he spent
his time in instructing his schoolmates in the path of devotion to the Lord
Vishnu.

When his father came to hear about it, he again became furious with
rage, and calling the boy to him, threatened to kill him, and abused Vishnu
in the worst language. But Prahlada still insisted that Vishnu was the Lord
of the universe, the Beginningless, the Endless, the Omnipotent and the
Omnipresent, and as such, he alone was to be worshipped. The king roared
with anger and said: "Thou evil one, if thy Vishnu is God omnipresent, why
doth he not reside in that pillar yonder?" Prahlada humbly submitted that
He did do so. "If so," cried the king, "let him defend thee; I will kill thee
with this sword." Thus saying the king rushed at him with sword in hand,
and dealt a terrible blow at the pillar. Instantly thundering voice was heard,
and lo and behold, there issued forth from the pillar Vishnu in His awful
Nrisimha form — half-lion, half-man! Panic-stricken, the Daityas ran away
in all directions; but Hiranyakashipu fought with him long and desperately,
till he was finally overpowered and killed.

Then the gods descended from heaven and offered hymns to Vishnu,
and Prahlada also fell at His feet and broke forth into exquisite hymns of
praise and devotion. And he heard the Voice of God saying, "Ask, Prahlada
ask for anything thou desires"; thou art My favourite child; therefore ask for

anything thou mayest wish." And Prahlada choked with feelings replied, "Lord, I have seen Thee. What else can I want? Do thou not tempt me with earthly or heavenly boons." Again the Voice said: "Yet ask something, my son." And then Prahlada replied, "That intense love, O Lord, which the ignorant bear to worldly things, may I have the same love for Thee; may I have the same intensity of love for Thee, but only for love's sake!"

Then the Lord said, "Prahlada, though My intense devotees never desire for anything, here or hereafter, yet by My command, do thou enjoy the blessings of this world to the end of the present cycle, and perform works of religious merit, with thy heart fixed on Me. And thus in time, after the dissolution of thy body, thou shalt attain Me." Thus blessing Prahlada, the Lord Vishnu disappeared. Then the gods headed by Brahma installed Prahlada on the throne of the Daityas and returned to their respective spheres.

The Great Teachers Of The World

(Delivered at the Shakespeare Club, Pasadena, California, February 3, 1900)

The universe, according to the theory of the Hindus, is moving in cycles of wave forms. It rises, reaches its zenith, then falls and remains in the hollow, as it were, for some time, once more to rise, and so on, in wave after wave and fall after fall. What is true of the universe is true of every part of it. The march of human affairs is like that. The history of nations is like that: they rise and they fall; after the rise comes a fall, again out of the fall comes a rise, with greater power. This motion is always going on. In the religious world the same movement exists. In every nation's spiritual life, there is a fall as well as a rise. The nation goes down, and everything seems to go to pieces. Then, again, it gains strength, rises; a huge wave comes, sometimes a tidal wave — and always on the topmost crest of the wave is a shining soul, the Messenger. Creator and created by turns, he is the impetus that makes the wave rise, the nation rise: at the same time, he is created by the same forces which make the wave, acting and interacting by turns. He puts forth his tremendous power upon society; and society makes him what he is. These are the great world-thinkers. These are the Prophets of the world, the Messengers of life, the Incarnations of God.

Man has an idea that there can be only one religion, that there can be only one Prophet, and that there can be only one Incarnation; but that idea is not true. By studying the lives of all these great Messengers, we find that each, as it were, was destined to play a part, and a part only; that the harmony consists in the sum total and not in one note. As in the life of races — no race is born to alone enjoy the world. None dare say no. Each race has a part to play in this divine harmony of nations. Each race has its mission to perform, its duty to fulfil. The sum total is the great harmony.

So, not any one of these Prophets is born to rule the world for ever. None has yet succeeded and none is going to be the ruler for ever. Each only contributes a part; and, as to that part, it is true that in the long run every Prophet will govern the world and its destinies.

Most of us are born believers in a personal religion. We talk of principles, we think of theories, and that is all right; but every thought and every movement, every one of our actions, shows that we can only understand the principle when it comes to us through a person. We can grasp an idea only when it comes to us through a materialised ideal person. We can understand the precept only through the example. Would to God that all of us were so developed that we would not require any example, would not require any person. But that we are not; and, naturally, the vast majority of mankind have put their souls at the feet of these extraordinary personalities, the Prophets, the Incarnations of God — Incarnations worshipped by the Christians, by the Buddhists, and by the Hindus. The Mohammedans from the beginning stood against any such worship. They would have nothing to do with worshipping the Prophets or the Messengers, or paying any homage to them; but, practically, instead of one Prophet, thousands upon thousands of saints are being worshipped. We cannot go against facts! We are bound to worship personalities, and it is good. Remember that word from your great Prophet to the query: "Lord, show us the Father", "He that hath seen me hath seen the Father." Which of us can imagine anything except that He is a man? We can only see Him in and through humanity. The vibration of light is everywhere in this room: why cannot lie see it everywhere? You have to see it only in that lamp. God is an Omnipresent Principle — everywhere: but we are so constituted at present that we can see Him, feel Him, only in and through a human God. And when these great Lights come, then man realises God. And they come in a different way from what we come. We come as beggars; they come as Emperors. We come here like orphans, as people who have lost their way and do not know it. What are we to do? We do not know what is the meaning of our lives. We cannot realise it. Today we are doing one thing, tomorrow another. We are like little bits of straw rocking to and fro in water, like feathers blown about in a hurricane.

But, in the history of mankind, you will find that there come these Messengers, and that from their very birth their mission is found and formed. The whole plan is there, laid down; and you see them swerving not one inch from that. Because they come with a mission, they come with a message, they do not want to reason. Did you ever hear or read of these great Teachers, or Prophets, reasoning out what they taught? No, not one of them did so. They speak direct. Why should they reason? They see the Truth. And not only do they see it but they show it! If you ask me, "Is there any God ?" and I say "Yes", you immediately ask my grounds for saying so, and poor me has to exercise all his powers to provide you with some reason. If you had come to Christ and said, "Is there any God? " he would have said, "Yes"; and if you had asked, "Is there any proof?" he would have replied, "Behold the Lord! " And thus, you see, it is a direct perception, and not at all the ratiocination of reason. There is no groping in the dark, but there is the strength of direct vision. I see this table; no amount of reason

can take that faith from me. It is a direct perception. Such is their faith —
faith in their ideals, faith in their mission, faith in themselves, above all else.
The great shining Ones believe in themselves as nobody else ever does. The
people say, "Do you believe in God? Do you believe in a future life? Do you
believe in this doctrine or that dogma?" But here the base is wanting: this
belief in oneself. Ay, the man who cannot believe in himself, how can they
expect him to believe in anything else? I am not sure of my own existence.
One moment I think that I am existing and nothing can destroy me; the next
moment I am quaking in fear of death. One minute I think I am immortal;
the next minute, a spook appears, and then I don't know what I am, nor
where I am. I don't know whether I am living or dead. One moment I think
that I am spiritual, that I am moral; and the next moment, a blow comes, and
I am thrown flat on my back. And why? — I have lost faith in myself, my
moral backbone is broken.

But in these great Teachers you will always find this sign: that they
have intense faith in themselves. Such intense faith is unique, and we cannot
understand it. That is why we try to explain away in various ways what
these Teachers speak of themselves; and people invent twenty thousand
theories to explain what they say about their realisation. We do not think
of ourselves in the same way, and, naturally, we cannot understand them.

Then again, when they speak, the world is bound to listen. When
they speak, each word is direct; it bursts like a bomb-shell. What is in the
word, unless it has the Power behind? What matters it what language you
speak, and how you arrange your language? What matters it whether you
speak correct grammar or with fine rhetoric? What matters it whether your
language is ornamental or not? The question is whether or not you have
anything to give. It is a question of giving and taking, and not listening.
Have you anything to give? — that is the first question. If you have, then
give. Words but convey the gift: it is but one of the many modes. Sometimes
we do not speak at all. There is an old Sanskrit verse which says, "I saw
the Teacher sitting under a tree. He was a young man of sixteen, and the
disciple was an old man of eighty. The preaching of the Teacher was silence,
and the doubts of the disciple departed."

Sometimes they do not speak at all, but yet they convey the Truth from
mind to mind. They come to give. They command, they are the Messengers;
you have to receive the Command. Do you not remember in your own
scriptures the authority with which Jesus speaks? "Go ye, therefore, and
teach all nations . . . teaching them to observe all things whatsoever I have
commanded you." It runs through all his utterances, that tremendous faith
in his own message. That you find in the life of all these great giants whom
the world worships as its Prophets.

These great Teachers are the living Gods on this earth. Whom else should we worship? I try to get an idea of God in my mind, and I find what a false little thing I conceive; it would be a sin to worship that God. I open my eyes and look at the actual life of these great ones of the earth. They are higher than any conception of God that I could ever form. For, what conception of mercy could a man like me form who would go after a man if he steals anything from me and send him to jail? And what can be my highest idea of forgiveness? Nothing beyond myself. Which of you can jump out of your own bodies? Which of you can jump out of your own minds? Not one of you. What idea of divine love can you form except what you actually live? What we have never experienced we can form no idea of. So, all my best attempts at forming an idea of God would fail in every case. And here are plain facts, and not idealism — actual facts of love, of mercy, of purity, of which I can have no conception even. What wonder that I should fall at the feet of these men and worship them as God? And what else can anyone do? I should like to see the man who can do anything else, however much he may talk. Talking is not actuality. Talking about God and the Impersonal, and this and that is all very good; but these man-Gods are the real Gods of all nations and all races. These divine men have been worshipped and will be worshipped so long as man is man. Therein is our faith, therein is our hope, of a reality. Of what avail is a mere mystical principle!

The purpose and intent of what I have to say to you is this, that I have found it possible in my life to worship all of them, and to be ready for all that are yet to come. A mother recognises her son in any dress in which he may appear before her; and if one does not do so, I am sure she is not the mother of that man. Now, as regards those of you that think that you understand Truth and Divinity and God in only one Prophet in the world, and not in any other, naturally, the conclusion which I draw is that you do not understand Divinity in anybody; you have simply swallowed words and identified yourself with one sect, just as you would in party politics, as a matter of opinion; but that is no religion at all. There are some fools in this world who use brackish water although there is excellent sweet water near by, because, they say, the brackish-water well was dug by their father. Now, in my little experience I have collected this knowledge — that for all the devilry that religion is, blamed with, religion is not at all in fault: no religion ever persecuted men, no religion ever burnt witches, no religion ever did any of these things. What then incited people to do these things? Politics, but never religion; and if such politics takes the name of religion whose fault is that?

So, when each man stands and says "My Prophet is the only true Prophet," he is not correct — he knows not the alpha of religion. Religion is neither talk, nor theory, nor intellectual consent. It is realisation in the heart of our hearts; it is touching God; it is feeling, realising that I am a spirit in relation with the Universal Spirit and all Its great manifestations. If you have really entered the house of the Father, how can you have seen His children and not known them? And if you do not recognise them, you have not entered the house of the Father. The mother recognises her child in any dress and knows him however disguised. Recognise all the great, spiritual men and women in every age and country, and see that they are not really at variance with one another. Wherever there has been actual religion — this touch of the Divine, the soul coming in direct sense-contact with the Divine — there has always been a broadening of the mind which enables it to see the light everywhere. Now, some Mohammedans are the crudest in this respect, and the most sectarian. Their watchword is: "There is one God, and Mohammed is His Prophet." Everything beyond that not only is bad, but must be destroyed forthwith; at a moment's notice, every man or woman who does not exactly believe in that must be killed; everything that does not belong to this worship must be immediately broken; every book that teaches any thing else must be burnt. From the Pacific to the Atlantic, for five hundred years blood ran all over the world. That is Mohammedanism! Nevertheless, among these Mohammedans, wherever there has a philosophic man, he was sure to protest against these cruelties. In that he showed the touch of the Divine and realised a fragment of the truth; he was not playing with his religion; for it was not his father's religion he was talking, but spoke the truth direct like a man.

Side by side with tie modern theory of evolution, there is another thing: atavism. There is a tendency in us to revert to old ideas in religion. Let us think something new, even if it be wrong. It is better to do that. Why should you not try to hit the mark? We become wiser through failures. Time is infinite. Look at the wall. Did the wall ever tell a lie? It is always the wall. Man tells a lie — and becomes a god too. It is better to do something; never mind even if it proves to be wrong it is better than doing nothing. The cow never tells a lie, but she remains a cow, all the time. Do something! Think some thought; it doesn't matter whether you are right or wrong. But think something! Because my forefathers did not think this way, shall I sit down quietly and gradually lose my sense of feeling and my own thinking faculties? I may as well be dead! And what is life worth if we have no living ideas, no convictions of our own about religion? There is some hope for the atheists, because though they differ from others, they think for themselves. The people who never think anything for themselves are not yet born into the world of religion; they have a mere jelly-fish existence. They will not think; they do not care for religion. But the disbeliever, the atheist, cares, and he is struggling. So think something! Struggle Godward! Never mind if you fail, never mind if you get hold of a queer theory. If you are afraid to be called queer, keep it in your own mind — you need not go and preach it to others. But do something! Struggle Godward! Light must come. If a man feeds me every day of my life, in the long run I shall lose the use of my hands. Spiritual death is the result of following each other like a flock of sheep. Death is the result of inaction. Be active; and wherever there is activity, there must be difference. Difference is the sauce of life; it is the beauty, it is the art of everything. Difference makes all beautiful here. It is variety that is the source of life, the sign of life. Why should we be afraid of it?

Now, we are coming into a position to understand about the Prophets. Now, we see that the historical evidence is — apart from the jelly-fish existence in religion — that where there has been any real thinking, any real love for God, the soul has grown Godwards and has got as it were, a glimpse now and then, has come into direct perception, even for a second, even once in its life. Immediately, "All doubts vanish for ever, and all the crookedness of the heart is made straight, and all bondages vanish, and the results of action and Karma fly when He is seen who is the nearest of the near and the farthest of the far." That is religion, that is all of religion; the rest is mere theory, dogma, so many ways of going to that state of direct perception. Now we are fighting over the basket and the fruits have fallen into the ditch.

If two men quarrel about religion, just ask them the question: "Have you seen God? Have you seen these things?" One man says that Christ is the only Prophet: well, has he seen Christ? "Has your father seen Him?" "No, Sir." "Has your grandfather seen Him?" "No, Sir." "Have you seen Him?" "No, Sir." "Then what are you quarrelling for? The fruits have fallen into the ditch, and you are quarrelling over the basket!" Sensible men and women should be ashamed to go on quarrelling in that way!

These great Messengers and Prophets are great and true. Why? Because, each one has come to preach a great idea. Take the Prophets of India, for instance. They are the oldest of the founders of religion. We takes first, Krishna. You who have read the Gitâ see all through the book that the one idea is non-attachment. Remain unattached. The heart's love is due to only

One. To whom? To Him who never changeth. Who is that One? It is God. Do not make the mistake of giving the heart to anything that is changing, because that is misery. You may give it to a man; but if he dies, misery is the result. You may give it to a friend, but he may tomorrow become your enemy. If you give it to your husband, he may one day quarrel with you. You may give it to your wife, and she may die the day after tomorrow. Now, this is the way the world is going on. So says Krishna in the Gita: The Lord is the only One who never changes. His love never fails. Wherever we are and whatever we do, He is ever and ever the same merciful, the same loving heart. He never changes, He is never angry, whatever we do. How can God be angry with us? Your babe does many mischievous things: are you angry with that babe? Does not God know what we are going to be? He knows we are all going to be perfect, sooner or later. He has patience, infinite patience. We must love Him, and everyone that lives — only in and through Him. This is the keynote. You must love the wife, but not for the wife's sake. "Never, O Beloved, is the husband loved on account of the husband, but because the Lord is in the husband." The Vedanta philosophy says that even in the love of the husband and wife, although the wife is thinking that she is loving the husband, the real attraction is the Lord, who is present there. He is the only attraction, there is no other; but the wife in most cases does not know that it is so, but ignorantly she is doing the right thing, which is, loving the Lord. Only, when one does it ignorantly, it may bring pain. If one does it knowingly, that is salvation. This is what our scriptures say. Wherever there is love, wherever there is a spark of joy, know that to be a spark of His presence because He is joy, blessedness, and love itself. Without that there cannot be any love.

This is the trend of Krishna's instruction all the time. He has implanted that upon his race, so that when a Hindu does anything, even if he drinks water, he says "If there is virtue in it, let it go to the Lord." The Buddhist says, if he does any good deed, "Let the merit of the good deed belong to the world; if there is any virtue in what I do, let it go to the world, and let the evils of the world come to me." The Hindu says he is a great believer in God; the Hindu says that God is omnipotent and that He is the Soul of every soul everywhere; the Hindu says, If I give all my virtues unto Him, that is the greatest sacrifice, and they will go to the whole universe."

Now, this is one phase; and what is the other message of Krishna? "Whosoever lives in the midst of the world, and works, and gives up all the fruit of his action unto the Lord, he is never touched with the evils of the world. Just as the lotus, born under the water, rises up and blossoms above the water, even so is the man who is engaged in the activities of the world, giving up all the fruit of his activities unto the Lord" (Gita, V. 10).

Krishna strikes another note as a teacher of intense activity. Work, work, work day and night, says the Gita. You may ask, "Then, where is peace? If all through life I am to work like a cart-horse and die in harness, what am I here for?" Krishna says, "Yes, you will find peace. Flying from work is never the way to find peace." Throw off your duties if you can, and go to the top of a mountain; even there the mind is going — whirling, whirling, whirling. Someone asked a Sannyasin, "Sir, have you found a nice place? How many years have you been travelling in the Himalayas?" "For forty years," replied the Sannyasin. "There are many beautiful spots to select from, and to settle down in: why did you not do so?" "Because for these forty years my mind would not allow me to do so." We all say, "Let us find peace"; but the mind will not allow us to do so.

You know the story of the man who caught a Tartar. A soldier was outside the town, and he cried out when be came near the barracks, "I have caught a Tartar." A voice called out, "Bring him in." "He won't come in, sir." "Then you come in." "He won't let me come in, sir." So, in this mind of ours, we have "caught a Tartar": neither can we tone it down, nor will it let us be toned down. We have all "caught Tartars". We all say, be quiet, and peaceful, and so forth. But every baby can say that and thinks he can do it. However, that is very difficult. I have tried. I threw overboard all my duties and fled to the tops of mountains; I lived in caves and deep forests — but all the same, I "caught a Tartar" because I had my world with me all the time. The "Tartar" is what I have in my own mind, so we must not blame poor people outside. "These circumstances are good, and these are bad," so we say, while the "Tartar" is here, within; if we can quiet him down, we shall be all right.

Therefore Krishna teaches us not to shirk our duties, but to take them up manfully, and not think of the result. The servant has no right to question. The soldier has no right to reason. Go forward, and do not pay too much attention to the nature of the work you have to do. Ask your mind if you are unselfish. If you are, never mind anything, nothing can resist you! Plunge in! Do the duty at hand. And when you have done this, by degrees you will realise the Truth: "Whosoever in the midst of intense activity finds intense peace, whosoever in the midst of the greatest peace finds the greatest activity, he is a Yogi, he is a great soul, he has arrived at perfection."

Now, you see that the result of this teaching is that all the duties of the world are sanctified. There is no duty in this world which we have any right to call menial: and each man's work is quite as good as that of the emperor on his throne.

Listen to Buddha's message — a tremendous message. It has a place in our heart. Says Buddha, "Root out selfishness, and everything that makes you selfish. Have neither wife, child, nor family. Be not of the world; become perfectly unselfish." A worldly man thinks he will be unselfish, but when he looks at the face of his wife it makes him selfish. The mother thinks she will be perfectly unselfish, but she looks at her baby, and immediately selfishness comes. So with everything in this world. As soon as selfish desires arise, as soon as some selfish pursuit is followed, immediately the whole man, the real man, is gone: he is like a brute, he is a slave' he forgets his fellow men. No more does he say, "You first and I afterwards," but it is "I first and let everyone else look out for himself."

We find that Krishna's message has also a place for us. Without that message, we cannot move at all. We cannot conscientiously and with peace, joy, and happiness, take up any duty of our lives without listening to the message of Krishna: "Be not afraid even if there is evil in your work, for there is no work which has no evil." "Leave it unto the Lord, and do not look for the results."

On the other hand, there is a corner in the heart for the other message: Time flies; this world is finite and all misery. With your good food, nice clothes, and your comfortable home, O sleeping man and woman, do you ever think of the millions that are starving and dying? Think of the great fact that it is all misery, misery, misery! Note the first utterance of the child: when it enters into the world, it weeps. That is the fact — the child-weeps. This is a place for weeping! If we listen to the Messenger, we should not be selfish.

Behold another Messenger, He of Nazareth. He teaches, "Be ready, for the Kingdom of Heaven is at hand." I have pondered over the message of Krishna, and am trying to work without attachment, but sometimes I forget. Then, suddenly, comes to me the message of Buddha: "Take care, for everything in the world as evanescent, and there is always misery in this life." I listen to that, and I am uncertain which to accept. Then again comes, like a thunderbolt, the message: "Be ready, for the Kingdom of Heaven is at hand." Do not delay a moment. Leave nothing for tomorrow. Get ready for the final event, which may overtake you immediately, even now. That message, also, has a place, and we acknowledge it. We salute the Messenger, we salute the Lord.

And then comes Mohammed, the Messenger of equality. You ask, "What good can there be in his religion?" If there were no good, how could it live? The good alone lives, that alone survives; because the good alone is strong, therefore it survives. How long is the life of an impure man, even in this life? Is not the life of the pure man much longer? Without doubt, for purity is strength, goodness is strength. How could Mohammedanism have lived, had there been nothing good in its teaching? There is much good. Mohammed was the Prophet of equality, of the brotherhood of man, the brotherhood of all Mussulmans

So we see that each Prophet, each Messenger, has a particular message. When you first listen to that message, and then look at his life, you see his whole life stands explained, radiant.

Now, ignorant fools start twenty thousand theories, and put forward, according to their own mental development, explanations to suit their own ideas, and ascribe them to these great Teachers. They take their teachings and put their misconstruction upon them. With every great Prophet his life is the only commentary. Look at his life: what he did will bear out the texts. Read the Gita, and you will find that it is exactly borne out by the life of the Teacher.

Mohammed by his life showed that amongst Mohammedans there should be perfect equality and brotherhood. There was no question of race, caste, creed, colour, or sex. The Sultan of Turkey may buy a Negro from the mart of Africa, and bring him in chains to Turkey; but should he become a Mohammedan and have sufficient merit and abilities, he might even marry the daughter of the Sultan. Compare this with the way in which the Negroes and the American Indians are treated in this country! And what do Hindus do? If one of your missionaries chance to touch the food of an orthodox person, he would throw it away. Notwithstanding our grand philosophy, you note our weakness in practice; but there You see the greatness of the Mohammedan beyond other races, showing itself in equality, perfect equality regardless of race or colour.

Will other and greater Prophets come? Certainly they will come in this world. But do not look forward to that. I should better like that each one of you became a Prophet of this real New Testament, which is made up of all the Old Testaments. Take all the old messages, supplement them with your own realisations, and become a Prophet unto others. Each one of these Teachers has been great; each has left something for us; they have been our Gods. We salute them, we are their servants; and, all the same, we salute ourselves; for if they have been Prophets and children of God, we also are the same. They reached their perfection, and we are going to attain ours now. Remember the words of Jesus: "The Kingdom of Heaven is at hand!" This very moment let everyone of us make a staunch resolution: "I will become a Prophet, I will become a messenger of Light, I will become a child of God, nay, I will become a God!"

On Lord Buddha

In every religion we find one type of self-devotion particularly developed. The type of working without a motive is most highly developed in Buddhism. Do not mistake Buddhism and Brâhminism. In this country you are very apt to do so. Buddhism is one of our sects. It was founded by a great man called Gautama, who became disgusted at the eternal metaphysical discussions of his day, and the cumbrous rituals, and more especially with the caste system. Some people say that we are born to a certain state, and therefore we are superior to others who are not thus born. He was also against the tremendous priestcraft. He preached a religion in which there was no motive power, and was perfectly agnostic about metaphysics or theories about God. He was often asked if there was a God, and he answered, he did not know. When asked about right conduct, he would reply, "Do good and be good." There came five Brâhmins, who asked him to settle their discussion. One said, "Sir, my book says that God is such and such, and that this is the way to come to God." Another said, "That is wrong, for my book says such and such, and this is the way to come to God"; and so the others. He listened calmly to all of them, and then asked them one by one, "Does any one of your books say that God becomes angry, that He ever injures anyone, that He is impure?" "No, Sir, they all teach that God is pure and good." "Then, my friends, why do you not become pure and good first, that you may know what God is?"

Of course I do not endorse all his philosophy. I want a good deal of metaphysics, for myself. I entirely differ in many respects, but, because I differ, is that any reason why I should not see the beauty of the man? He was the only man who was bereft of all motive power. There were other great men who all said they were the Incarnations of God Himself, and that those who would believe in them would go to heaven. But what did Buddha say with his dying breath? "None can help you; help yourself; work out your own salvation." He said about himself, "Buddha is the name of infinite knowledge, infinite as the sky; I, Gautama, have reached that state; you will all reach that too if you struggle for it." Bereft of all motive power, he did not want to go to heaven, did not want money; he gave up his throne and everything else and went about begging his bread through the streets of India, preaching for the good of men and animals with a heart as wide as the ocean.

He was the only man who was ever ready to give up his life for animals to stop a sacrifice. He once said to a king, "If the sacrifice of a lamb helps you to go to heaven, sacrificing a man will help you better; so sacrifice me." The king was astonished. And yet this man was without any motive power. He stands as the perfection of the active type, and the very height to which he attained shows that through the power of work we can also attain to the highest spirituality.

To many the path becomes easier if they believe in God. But the life of Buddha shows that even a man who does not believe in God, has no metaphysics, belongs to no sect, and does not go to any church, or temple, and is a confessed materialist, even he can attain to the highest. We have no right to judge him. I wish I had one infinitesimal part of Buddha's heart. Buddha may or may not have believed in God; that does not matter to me. He reached the same state of perfection to which others come by Bhakti — love of God — Yoga, or Jnâna. Perfection does not come from belief or faith. Talk does not count for anything. Parrots can do that. Perfection comes through the disinterested performance of action.

Christ, The Messenger

(Delivered at Los Angeles, California, 1900)

The wave rises on the ocean, and there is a hollow. Again another wave rises, perhaps bigger than the former, to fall down again, similarly, again to rise — driving onward. In the march of events, we notice the rise and fall, and we generally look towards the rise, forgetting the fall. But both are necessary, and both are great. This is the nature of the universe. Whether in the world of our thoughts, the world of our relations in society, or in our spiritual affairs, the same movement of succession, of rises and falls, is going on. Hence great predominances in the march of events, the liberal ideals, are marshalled ahead, to sink down, to digest, as it were, to ruminate over the past — to adjust, to conserve, to gather strength once more for a rise and a bigger rise.

The history of nations also has ever been like that. The great soul, the Messenger we are to study this afternoon, came at a period of the history of his race which we may well designate as a great fall. We catch only little glimpses here and there of the stray records that have been kept of his sayings and doings; for verily it has been well said, that the doings and sayings of that great soul would fill the world if they had all been written down. And the three years of his ministry were like one compressed, concentrated age, which it has taken nineteen hundred years to unfold, and who knows how much longer it will yet take! Little men like you and me are simply the recipients of just a little energy. A few minutes, a few hours, a few years at best, are enough to spend it all, to stretch it out, as it were, to its fullest strength, and then we are gone for ever. But mark this giant that came; centuries and ages pass, yet the energy that he left upon the world is not yet stretched, nor yet expended to its full. It goes on adding new vigour as the ages roll on.

Now what you see in the life of Christ is the life of all the past. The life of every man is, in a manner, the life of the past. It comes to him through heredity, through surroundings, through education, through his own reincarnation — the past of the race. In a manner, the past of the earth, the past of the whole world is there, upon every soul. What are we, in the present, but a result, an effect, in the hands of that infinite past? What are we but floating waveless in the eternal current of events, irresistibly moved forward and onward and incapable of rest? But you and I are only little things, bubbles. There are always some giant waves in the ocean of affairs, and in you and me the life of the past race has been embodied only a little; but there are giants who embody, as it were, almost the whole of the past and who stretch out their hands for the future. These are the sign-posts here and there which point to the march of humanity; these are verily gigantic, their shadows covering the earth — they stand undying, eternal! As it has been said by the same Messenger, "No man hath seen God at any time, but through the Son." And that is true. And where shall we see God but in the Son? It is true that you and I, and the poorest of us, the meanest even, embody that God, even reflect that God. The vibration of light is everywhere, omnipresent; but we have to strike the light of the lamp before we can see the light. The Omnipresent God of the universe cannot be seen until He is reflected by these giant lamps of the earth — The Prophets, the man-Gods, the Incarnations, the embodiments of God.

We all know that God exists, and yet we do not see Him, we do not understand Him. Take one of these great Messengers of light, compare his character with the highest ideal of God that you ever formed, and you will find that your God falls short of the ideal, and that the character of the Prophet exceeds your conceptions. You cannot even form a higher ideal of God than what the actually embodied have practically realised and set before us as an example. Is it wrong, therefore, to worship these as God? Is it a sin to fall at the feet of these man-Gods and worship them as the only divine beings in the world? If they are really, actually, higher than all our conceptions of God, what harm is there in worshipping them? Not only is there no harm, but it is the only possible and positive way of worship. However much you may try by struggle, by abstraction, by whatsoever method you like, still so long as you are a man in the world of men, your world is human, your religion is human, and your God is human. And that must be so. Who is not practical enough to take up an actually existing thing and give up an idea which is only an abstraction, which he cannot grasp, and is difficult of approach except through a concrete medium? Therefore, these Incarnations of God have been worshipped in all ages and in all countries.

We are now going to study a little of the life of Christ, the Incarnation of the Jews. When Christ was born, the Jews were in that state which I call a state of fall between two waves; a state of conservatism; a state where the human mind is, as it were, tired for the time being of moving forward and is taking care only of what it has already; a state when the attention is more bent upon particulars, upon details, than upon the great, general, and bigger problems of life; a state of stagnation, rather than a towing ahead; a state of suffering more than of doing. Mark you, I do not blame this state of things. We have no right to criticise it — because had it not been for this fall, the next rise, which was embodied in Jesus of Nazareth would have been impossible. The Pharisees and Sadducees might have been insincere, they might have been doing things which they ought not to have done; they might have been even hypocrites; but whatever they were, these factors were the very cause, of which the Messenger was the effect. The Pharisees and Sadducees at one end were the very impetus which came out at the other end as the gigantic brain of Jesus of Nazareth.

The attention to forms, to formulas, to the everyday details of religion, and to rituals, may sometimes be laughed at; but nevertheless, within them is strength. Many times in the rushing forward we lose much strength. As a fact, the fanatic is stronger than the liberal man. Even the fanatic, therefore, has one great virtue, he conserves energy, a tremendous amount of it. As with the individual so with the race, energy is gathered to be conserved. Hemmed in all around by external enemies, driven to focus in a centre by the Romans, by the Hellenic tendencies in the world of intellect, by waves from Persia, India, and Alexandria — hemmed in physically, mentally, and morally — there stood the race with an inherent, conservative, tremendous strength, which their descendants have not lost even today. And the race was forced to concentrate and focus all its energies upon Jerusalem and Judaism. But all power when once gathered cannot remain collected; it must expend and expand itself. There is no power on earth which can be kept long confined within a narrow limit. It cannot be kept compressed too long to allow of expansion at a subsequent period.

This concentrated energy amongst the Jewish race found its expression at the next period in the rise of Christianity. The gathered streams collected into a body. Gradually, all the little streams joined together, and became a surging wave on the top of which we find standing out the character of Jesus of Nazareth. Thus, every Prophet is a creation of his own times, the creation of the past of his race; he himself is the creator of the future. The cause of today is the effect of the past and the cause for the future. In this position stands the Messenger. In him is embodied all that is the best and greatest in his own race, the meaning, the life, for which that race has struggled for ages; and he himself is the impetus for the future, not only to his own race but to unnumbered other races of the world.

We must bear another fact in mind: that my view of the great Prophet of Nazareth would be from the standpoint of the Orient. Many times you forget, also, that the Nazarene himself was an Oriental of Orientals. With all your attempts to paint him with blue eyes and yellow hair, the Nazarene was still an Oriental. All the similes, the imageries, in which the Bible is written — the scenes, the locations, the attitudes, the groups, the poetry, and symbol, — speak to you of the Orient: of the bright sky, of the heat, of the sun, of the desert, of the thirsty men and animals; of men and women coming with pitchers on their heads to fill them at the wells; of the flocks, of the ploughmen, of the cultivation that is going on around; of the water-mill and wheel, of the mill-pond, of the millstones. All these are to be seen today in Asia.

The voice of Asia has been the voice of religion. The voice of Europe is the voice of politics. Each is great in its own sphere. The voice of Europe is the voice of ancient Greece. To the Greek mind, his immediate society was all in all: beyond that, it is Barbarian. None but the Greek has the right to live. Whatever the Greeks do is right and correct; whatever else there exists in the world is neither right nor correct, nor should be allowed to live. It is intensely human in its sympathies, intensely natural, intensely artistic, therefore. The Greek lives entirely in this world. He does not care to dream. Even his poetry is practical. His gods and goddesses are not only human beings, but intensely human, with all human passions and feelings almost the same as with any of us. He loves what is beautiful, but, mind you, it is always external nature: the beauty of the hills, of the snows, of the flowers, the beauty of forms and of figures, the beauty in the human face, and, more often, in the human form — that is what the Greeks liked. And the Greeks being the teachers of all subsequent Europeanism, the voice of Europe is Greek.

There is another type in Asia. Think of that vast, huge continent, whose mountain-tops go beyond the clouds, almost touching the canopy of heaven's blue; a rolling desert of miles upon miles where a drop of water cannot be found, neither will a blade of grass grow; interminable forests and gigantic rivers rushing down into the sea. In the midst of all these surroundings, the oriental love of the beautiful and of the sublime developed itself in another direction. It looked inside, and not outside. There is also the thirst for nature, and there is also the same thirst for power; there is also the same thirst for excellence, the same idea of the Greek and Barbarian, but it has extended over a larger circle. In Asia, even today, birth or colour or language never makes a race. That which makes a race is its religion. We are all Christians; we are all Mohammedans; we are all Hindus, or all Buddhists. No matter if a Buddhist is a Chinaman, or is a man from Persia, they think that they are brothers, because of their professing the same religion. Religion is the tie, unity of humanity. And then again, the Oriental, for the same reason, is a visionary, is a born dreamer. The ripples of the waterfalls, the songs of the birds, the beauties of the sun and moon and the stars and the whole earth are pleasant enough; but they are not sufficient for the oriental mind;

He wants to dream a dream beyond. He wants to go beyond the present. The present, as it were, is nothing to him. The Orient has been the cradle of the human race for ages, and all the vicissitudes of fortune are there — kingdoms succeeding kingdoms, empires succeeding empires, human power, glory, and wealth, all rolling down there: a Golgotha of power and learning. That is the Orient: a Golgotha of power, of kingdoms, of learning. No wonder, the oriental mind looks with contempt upon the things of this world and naturally wants to see something that changeth not, something which dieth not, something which in the midst of this world of misery and death is eternal, blissful, undying. An oriental Prophet never tires of insisting upon these ideals; and, as for Prophets, you may also remember that without one exception, all the Messengers were Orientals.

We see, therefore, in the life of this area: Messenger of life, the first watchword: "Not this life, but something higher"; and, like the true son of the Orient, he is practical in that. You people of the West are practical in your own department, in military affairs, and in managing political circles and other things. Perhaps the Oriental is not practical in those ways, but he is practical in his own field; he is practical in religion. If one preaches a philosophy, tomorrow there are hundreds who will struggle their best to make it practical in their lives. If a man preaches that standing on one foot would lead one to salvation, he will immediately get five hundred to stand on one foot. You may call it ludicrous; but, mark you, beneath that is their philosophy — that intense practicality. In the West, plans of salvation mean intellectual gymnastics — plans which are never worked out, never brought into practical life. In the West, the preacher who talks the best is the greatest preacher.

So, we find Jesus of Nazareth, in the first place, the true son of the Orient, intensely practical. He has no faith in this evanescent world and all its belongings. No need of text-torturing, as is the fashion in the West in modern times, no need of stretching out texts until the, will not stretch any more. Texts are not India rubber, and even that has its limits. Now, no making of religion to pander to the sense vanity of the present day! Mark you, let us all be honest. If we cannot follow the ideal, let us confess our weakness, but not degrade it; let not any try to pull it down. One gets sick at heart at the different accounts of the life of the Christ that Western people give. I do not know what he was or what he was not! One would make him a great politician; another, perhaps, would make of him a great military general; another, a great patriotic Jew; and so on. Is there any warrant in the books for all such assumptions? The best commentary on the life of a great teacher is his own life. "The foxes have holes, the birds of the air have nests, but the Son of man hath not where to lay his head." That is what Christ says as they only way to salvation; he lays down no other way. Let us confess in sackcloth and ashes that we cannot do that. We still have fondness for "me and mine". We want property, money, wealth. Woe unto us! Let us confess and not put to shame that great Teacher of Humanity! He had no family ties. But do you think that, that Man had any physical ideas in him? Do you think that, this mass of light, this God and not-man, came down to earth, to be the brother of animals? And yet, people make him preach all sorts of things. He had no sex ideas! He was a soul! Nothing but a soul — just working a body for the good of humanity; and that was all his relation to the body. In the soul there is no sex. The disembodied soul has no relationship to the animal, no relationship to the body. The ideal may be far away beyond us. But never mind, keep to the ideal. Let us confess that it is our ideal, but we cannot approach it yet.

He had no other occupation in life, no other thought except that one, that he was a spirit. He was a disembodied, unfettered, unbound spirit. And not only so, but he, with his marvellous vision, had found that every man and woman, whether Jew or Gentile, whether rich or poor, whether saint or sinner, was the embodiment of the same undying spirit as himself. Therefore, the one work his whole life showed was to call upon them to realise their own spiritual nature. Give up, he says, these superstitious dreams that you are low and that you are poor. Think not that you are trampled upon and tyrannised over as if you were slaves, for within you is something that can never be tyrannised over, never be trampled upon, never be troubled, never be killed. You are all Sons of God, immortal spirit. "Know", he declared, "the Kingdom of Heaven is within you." "I and my Father are one." Dare you stand up and say, not only that "I am the Son of God", but I shall also find in my heart of hearts that "I and my Father are one"? That was what Jesus of Nazareth said. He never talks of this world and of this life. He has nothing to do with it, except that he wants to get hold of the world as it is, give it a push and drive it forward and onward until the whole world has reached to the effulgent Light of God, until everyone has realised his spiritual nature, until death is vanished and misery banished.

We have read the different stories that have been written about him; we know the scholars and their writings, and the higher criticism; and we know all that has been done by study. We are not here to discuss how much of the New Testament is true, we are not here to discuss how much of that life is historical. It does not matter at all whether the New Testament was written within five hundred years of his birth, nor does it matter even, how much of that life is true. But there is something behind it, something we want to imitate. To tell a lie, you have to imitate a truth, and that truth is a fact. You cannot imitate that which never existed. You cannot imitate that which you never perceived. But there must have been a nucleus, a tremendous power that came down, a marvellous manifestation of spiritual power — and of that we are speaking. It stands there. Therefore, we are not afraid of all the criticisms of the scholars. If I, as an Oriental, have to worship Jesus of Nazareth, there is only one way left to me, that is, to worship him as God and nothing else. Have we no right to worship him in that way, do you mean to say? If we bring him down to our own level and simply pay him a little respect as a great man, why should we worship at all? Our scriptures say, "These great children of Light, who manifest the Light themselves, who are Light themselves, they, being worshipped, become, as it were, one with us and we become one with them."

For, you see, in three ways man perceives God. At first the undeveloped intellect of the uneducated man sees God as far away, up in the heavens somewhere, sitting on a throne as a great Judge. He looks upon Him as a fire, as a terror. Now, that is good, for there is nothing bad in it. You must remember that humanity travels not from error to truth, but from truth to truth; it may be, if you like it better, from lower truth to higher truth, but never from error to truth. Suppose you start from here and travel towards the sun in a straight line. From here the sun looks only small in size. Suppose you go forward a million miles, the sun will be much bigger. At every stage the sun will become bigger and bigger. Suppose twenty thousand photographs had been taken of the same sun, from different standpoints; these twenty thousand photographs will all certainly differ from one another. But can you deny that each is a photograph of the same sun? So all forms of religion, high or low, are just different stages toward that eternal state of Light, which is God Himself. Some embody a lower view, some a higher, and that is all the difference. Therefore, the religions of the unthinking masses all over the world must be, and have always been, of a God who is outside of the universe, who lives in heaven, who governs from that place, who is a punisher of the bad and a rewarder of the good, and so on. As man advanced spiritually, he began to feel that God was omnipresent, that He must be in him, that He must be everywhere, that He was not a distant God, but dearly the Soul of all souls. As my soul moves my body, even so is God the mover of my soul. Soul within soul. And a few individuals who had developed enough and were pure enough, went still further, and at last found God. As the New Testament says, "Blessed are the pure in heart, for they shall see God." And they found at last that they and the Father were one.

You find that all these three stages are taught by the Great Teacher in the New Testament. Note the Common Prayer he taught: "Our Father which art in Heaven, hallowed be Thy name," and so on — a simple prayer, a child's prayer. Mark you, it is the "Common Prayer" because it is intended for the uneducated masses. To a higher circle, to those who had advanced a little more, he gave a more elevated teaching: "I am in my Father, and ye in me, and I in you." Do you remember that? And then, when the Jews asked him who he was, he declared that he and his Father were one, and the Jews thought that that was blasphemy. What did he mean by that? This has been also told by your old Prophets, "Ye are gods and all of you are children of the Most High." Mark the same three stages. You will find that it is easier for you to begin with the first and end with the last.

The Messenger came to show the path: that the spirit is not in forms, that it is not through all sorts of vexations and knotty problems of philosophy that you know the spirit. Better that you had no learning, better that you never read a book in your life. These are not at all necessary for salvation — neither wealth, nor position nor power, not even learning; but what is necessary is that one thing, purity. "Blessed are the pure in heart," for the spirit in its own nature is pure. How can it be otherwise? It is of God, it has come from God. In the language of the Bible, "It is the breath of God." In the language of the Koran, "It is the soul of God." Do you mean to say that the Spirit of God can ever be impure? But, alas, it has been, as it were, covered over with the dust and dirt of ages, through our own actions, good and evil. Various works which were not correct, which were not true, have covered the same spirit with the dust and dirt of the ignorance of ages. It is only necessary to clear away the dust and dirt, and then the spirit shines immediately. "Blessed are the pure in heart, for they shall see God." "The Kingdom of Heaven is within you." Where goest thou to seek for the Kingdom of God, asks Jesus of Nazareth, when it is there, within you? Cleanse the spirit, and it is there. It is already yours. How can you get what is not yours? It is yours by right. You are the heirs of immortality, sons of the Eternal Father.

This is the great lesson of the Messenger, and another which is the basis of all religions, is renunciation. How can you make the spirit pure? By renunciation. A rich young man asked Jesus, "Good Master, what shall I do that I may inherit eternal life?" And Jesus said unto him, "One thing thou lackest; go thy way, sell whatsoever thou hast, and give to the poor, and thou shalt have treasures in heaven: and come, take up thy cross, and follow

Me." And he was sad at that saying and went away grieved; for he had great possessions. We are all more or less like that. The voice is ringing in our ears day and night. In the midst of our pleasures and joys, in the midst of worldly things, we think that we have forgotten everything else. Then comes a moment's pause and the voice rings in our ears "Give up all that thou hast and follow Me." "Whosoever will save his life shall lose it; and whosoever shall lose his life for My sake shall find it." For whoever gives up this life for His sake, finds the life immortal. In the midst of all our weakness there is a moment of pause and the voice rings: "Give up all that thou hast; give it to the poor and follow me." This is the one ideal he preaches, and this has been the ideal preached by all the great Prophets of the world: renunciation. What is meant by renunciation? That there is only one ideal in morality: unselfishness. Be selfless. The ideal is perfect unselfishness. When a man is struck on the right cheek, he turns the left also. When a man's coat is carried off, he gives away his cloak also.

We should work in the best way we can, without dragging the ideal down. Here is the ideal. When a man has no more self in him, no possession, nothing to call "me" or "mine", has given himself up entirely, destroyed himself as it were — in that man is God Himself; for in him self-will is gone, crushed out, annihilated. That is the ideal man. We cannot reach that state yet; yet, let us worship the ideal, and slowly struggle to reach the ideal, though, maybe, with faltering steps. It may be tomorrow, or it may be a thousand years hence; but that ideal has to be reached. For it is not only the end, but also the means. To be unselfish, perfectly selfless, is salvation itself; for the man within dies, and God alone remains.

One more point. All the teachers of humanity are unselfish. Suppose Jesus of Nazareth was teaching; and a man came and told him, "What you teach is beautiful. I believe that it is the way to perfection, and I am ready to follow it; but I do not care to worship you as the only begotten Son of God." What would be the answer of Jesus of Nazareth? "Very well, brother, follow the ideal and advance in your own way. I do not care whether you give me the credit for the teaching or not. I am not a shopkeeper. I do not trade in religion. I only teach truth, and truth is nobody's property. Nobody can patent truth. Truth is God Himself. Go forward." But what the disciples say nowadays is: "No matter whether you practise the teachings or not, do you give credit to the Man? If you credit the Master, you will be saved; if not, there is no salvation for you." And thus the whole teaching of the Master is degenerated, and all the struggle and fight is for the personality of the Man.

They do not know that in imposing that difference, they are, in a manner, bringing shame to the very Man they want to honour — the very Man that would have shrunk with shame from such an idea. What did he care if there was one man in the world that remembered him or not? He had to deliver his message, and he gave it. And if he had twenty thousand lives, he would give them all up for the poorest man in the world. If he had to be tortured millions of times for a million despised Samaritans, and if for each one of them the sacrifice of his own life would be the only condition of salvation, he would have given his life. And all this without wishing to have his name known even to a single person. Quiet, unknown, silent, would he world, just as the Lord works. Now, what would the disciple say? He will tell you that you may be a perfect man, perfectly unselfish; but unless you give the credit to our teacher, to our saint, it is of no avail. Why? What is the origin of this superstition, this ignorance? The disciple thinks that the Lord can manifest Himself only once. There lies the whole mistake. God manifests Himself to you in man. But throughout nature, what happens once must have happened before, and must happen in future. There is nothing in nature which is not bound by law; and that means that whatever happens once must go on and must have been going on.

In India they have the same idea of the Incarnations of God. One of their great Incarnations, Krishna, whose grand sermon, the Bhagavad-Gitâ, some of you might have read, says, "Though I am unborn, of changeless nature, and Lord of beings, yet subjugating My Prakriti, I come into being by My own Mâyâ. Whenever virtue subsides and immorality prevails, then I body Myself forth. For the protection of the good, for the destruction of the wicked, and for the establishment of Dharma, I come into being, in every age." Whenever the world goes down, the Lord comes to help it forward; and so He does from time to time and place to place. In another passage He speaks to this effect: Wherever thou findest a great soul of immense power and purity struggling to raise humanity, know that he is born of My splendour, that I am there working through him.

Let us, therefore, find God not only in Jesus of Nazareth, but in all the great Ones that have preceded him, in all that came after him, and all that are yet to come. Our worship is unbounded and free. They are all manifestations of the same Infinite God. They are all pure and unselfish; they struggled and gave up their lives for us, poor human beings. They each and all suffer vicarious atonement for every one of us, and also for all that are to come hereafter.

In a sense you are all Prophets; every one of you is a Prophet, bearing the burden of the world on your own shoulders. Have you ever seen a man, have you ever seen a woman, who is not quietly, patiently, bearing his or her little burden of life? The great Prophets were giants — they bore a gigantic world on their shoulders. Compared with them we are pigmies, no doubt, yet we are doing the same task; in our little circles, in our little homes, we are bearing our little crosses. There is no one so evil, no one so worthless, but he has to bear his own cross. But with all our mistakes, with all our evil thoughts and evil deeds, there is a bright spot somewhere, there is still somewhere the golden thread through which we are always in touch with the divine. For, know for certain, that the moment the touch of the divine is lost there would be annihilation. And because none can be annihilated, there is always somewhere in our heart of hearts, however low and degraded we may be, a little circle of light which is in constant touch with the divine.

Our salutations go to all the past Prophets whose teachings and lives we have inherited, whatever might have been their race, clime, or creed! Our salutations go to all those Godlike men and women who are working to help humanity, whatever be their birth, colour, or race! Our salutations to those who are coming in the future — living Gods — to work unselfishly for our descendants.

My Master

*(Two lectures delivered in New York and England in 1896
were combined subsequently under the present heading.)*

"Whenever virtue subsides and vice prevails, I come down to help mankind," declares Krishna, in the Bhagavad-Gitâ. Whenever this world of ours, on account of growth, on account of added circumstances, requires a new adjustment, a wave of power comes; and as a man is acting on two planes, the spiritual and the material, waves of adjustment come on both planes. On the one side, of the adjustment on the material plane, Europe has mainly been the basis during modern times; and of the adjustment on the other, the spiritual plane, Asia has been the basis throughout the history of the world. Today, man requires one more adjustment on the spiritual plane; today when material ideas are at the height of their glory and power, today when man is likely to forget his divine nature, through his growing dependence on matter, and is likely to be reduced to a mere money-making machine, an adjustment is necessary; the voice has spoken, and the power is coming to drive away the clouds of gathering materialism. The power has been set in motion which, at no distant date, will bring unto mankind once more the memory of its real nature; and again the place from which this power will start will be Asia.

This world of ours is on the plan of the division of labour. It is vain to say that one man shall possess everything. Yet how childish we are! The baby in its ignorance thinks that its doll is the only possession that is to be coveted in this whole universe. So a nation which is great in the possession of material power thinks that that is all that is to be coveted, that that is all that is meant by progress, that that is all that is meant by civilisation, and if there are other nations which do not care for possession and do not possess that power, they are not fit to live, their whole existence is useless! On the other hand, another nation may think that mere material civilisation is utterly useless. From the Orient came the voice which once told the world that if a man possesses everything that is under the sun and does not possess spirituality, what avails it? This is the oriental type; the other is the occidental type.

Each of these types has its grandeur, each has its glory. The present adjustment will be the harmonising, the mingling of these two ideals. To the Oriental, the world of spirit is as real as to the Occidental is the world of senses. In the spiritual, the Oriental finds everything he wants or hopes for; in it he finds all that makes life real to him. To the Occidental he is a dreamer; to the Oriental the Occidental is a dreamer playing with ephemeral toys, and he laughs to think that grown-up men and women should make so much of a handful of matter which they will have to leave sooner or later. Each calls the other a dreamer. But the oriental ideal is as necessary for the progress of the human race as is the occidental, and I think it is more necessary. Machines never made mankind happy and never will make. He who is trying to make us believe this will claim that happiness is in the machine; but it is always in the mind. That man alone who is the lord of his mind can become happy, and none else. And what, after all, is this power of machinery? Why should a man who can send a current of electricity through a wire be called a very great man and a very intelligent man? Does not nature do a million times more than that every moment? Why not then fall down and worship nature? What avails it if you have power over the whole of the world, if you have mastered every atom in the universe? That will not make you happy unless you have the power of happiness in yourself, until you have conquered yourself. Man is born to conquer nature, it is true, but the Occidental means by "nature" only physical or external nature. It is true that external nature is majestic, with its mountains, and oceans, and rivers, and with its infinite powers and varieties. Yet there is a more majestic internal nature of man, higher than the sun, moon, and stars, higher than this earth of ours, higher than the physical universe, transcending these little lives of ours; and it affords another field of study. There the Orientals excel, just as the Occidentals excel in the other. Therefore it is fitting that, whenever there is a spiritual adjustment, it should come from the Orient. It is also fitting that when the Oriental wants to learn about machine-making, he should sit at the feet of the Occidental and learn from him. When the Occident wants to learn about the spirit, about God, about the soul, about the meaning and the mystery of this universe, he must sit at the feet of the Orient to learn.

I am going to present before you the life of one man who has put in motion such a wave in India. But before going into the life of this man, I will try to present before you the secret of India, what India means. If those whose eyes have been blinded by the glamour of material things, whose whole dedication of life is to eating and drinking and enjoying, whose ideal of possession is lands and gold, whose ideal of pleasure is that of the senses, whose God is money, and whose goal is a life of ease and comfort in this world and death after that, whose minds never look forward, and who rarely think of anything higher than the sense-objects in the midst of which they live — if such as these go to India, what do they see? Poverty, squalor, superstition, darkness, hideousness everywhere. Why? Because in their minds enlightenment means dress, education, social politeness. Whereas occidental nations have used every effort to improve their material position, India has done differently. There live the only men in the world who, in the whole history of humanity, never went beyond their frontiers to conquer anyone, who never coveted that which belonged to anyone else, whose only fault was that their lands were so fertile, and they accumulated wealth by the hard labour of their hands, and so tempted other nations to come and despoil them. They are contented to be despoiled, and to be called barbarians; and in return they want to send to this world visions of the Supreme, to lay bare for the world the secrets of human nature, to rend the veil that conceals the real man, because they know the dream, because they know that behind this materialism lives the real, divine nature of man which no sin can tarnish, no crime can spoil, no lust can taint, which fire cannot burn, nor water wet, which heat cannot dry nor death kill. And to them this true nature of man is as real as is any material object to the senses of an Occidental.

Just as you are brave to jump at the mouth of a cannon with a hurrah, just as you are brave in the name of patriotism to stand up and give up your lives for your country, so are they brave in the name of God. There it is that when a man declares that this is a world of ideas, that it is all a dream, he casts off clothes and property to demonstrate that what he believes and thinks is true. There it is that a man sits on the bank of a river, when he has known that life is eternal, and wants to give up his body just as nothing, just as you can give up a bit of straw. Therein lies their heroism, that they are ready to face death as a brother, because they are convinced that there is no death for them. Therein lies the strength that has made them invincible through hundreds of years of oppression and foreign invasion and tyranny. The nation lives today, and in that nation even in the days of the direst disaster, spiritual giants have, never failed to arise. Asia produces giants in spirituality, just as the Occident produces giants in politics, giants in science. In the beginning of the present century, when Western influence began to pour into India, when Western conquerors, sword in hand, came to demonstrate to the children of the sages that they were mere barbarians, a race of dreamers, that their religion was but mythology, and god and soul and everything they had been struggling for were mere words without meaning, that the thousands of years of struggle, the thousands of years of endless renunciation, had all been in vain, the question began to be agitated among young men at the universities whether the whole national existence up to then had been a failure, whether they must begin anew on the occidental plan, tear up their old books, burn their philosophies, drive away their preachers, and break down their temples. Did not the occidental conqueror, the man who demonstrated his religion with sword and gun, say that all the old ways were mere superstition and idolatry? Children brought up and educated in the new schools started on the occidental plan, drank in these ideas, from their childhood; and it is not to be wondered at that doubts arose. But instead of throwing away superstition and making a real search after truth, the test of truth became, "What does the West say?" The priests must go, the Vedas must be burned, because the West has said so. Out of the feeling of unrest thus produced, there arose a wave of so-called reform in India.

If you wish to be a true reformer, three things are necessary. The first is to feel. Do you really feel for your brothers? Do you really feel that there is so much misery in the world, so much ignorance and superstition? Do you really feel that men are your brothers? Does this idea come into your whole being? Does it run with your blood? Does it tingle in your veins? Does it course through every nerve and filament of your body? Are you full of that idea of sympathy? If you are, that is only the first step. You must think next if you have found any remedy. The old ideas may be all superstition, but in and round these masses of superstition are nuggets of gold and truth. Have you discovered means by which to keep that gold alone, without any of the dross? If you have done that, that is only the second step; one more thing is necessary. What is your motive? Are you sure that you are not actuated by greed of gold, by thirst for fame or power? Are you really sure that you can stand to your ideals and work on, even if the whole world wants to crush you down? Are you sure you know what you want and will perform your duty, and that alone, even if your life is at stake? Are you sure that you will persevere so long as life endures, so long as there is one pulsation left in the heart? Then you are a real reformer, you are a teacher, a Master, a blessing to mankind. But man is so impatient, so short-sighted! He has not the patience to wait, he has not the power to see. He wants to rule, he wants results immediately. Why? He wants to reap the fruits himself, and does not really care for others. Duty for duty's sake is not what he wants. "To work you have the right, but not to the fruits thereof," says Krishna. Why cling to results? Ours are the duties. Let the fruits take care of themselves. But man has no patience. He takes up any scheme. The larger number of would-be reformers all over the world can be classed under this heading.

As I have said, the idea of reform came to India when it seemed as if the wave of materialism that had invaded her shores would sweep away the teachings of the sages. But the nation had borne the shocks of a thousand such waves of change. This one was mild in comparison. Wave after wave had flooded the land, breaking and crushing everything for hundreds of years. The sword had flashed, and "Victory unto Allah" had rent the skies of India; but these floods subsided, leaving the national ideals unchanged.

The Indian nation cannot be killed. Deathless it stands, and it will stand so long as that spirit shall remain as the background, so long as her people do not give up their spirituality. Beggars they may remain, poor and poverty-stricken, dirt and squalor may surround them perhaps throughout all time, but let them not give up their God, let them not forget that they are the children of the sages. Just as in the West, even the man in the street wants to trace his descent from some robber-baron of the Middle Ages, so in India, even an Emperor on the throne wants to trace his descent from some beggar-sage in the forest, from a man who wore the bark of a tree, lived upon the fruits of the forest and communed with God. That is the type of descent we want; and so long as holiness is thus supremely venerated, India cannot die.

Many of you perhaps have read the article by Prof. Max Müller in a recent issue of the *Nineteenth Century*, headed "A Real Mahâtman". The life of Shri Ramakrishna is interesting, as it was a living illustration of the ideas that he preached. Perhaps it will be a little romantic for you who live in the West in an atmosphere entirely different from that of India. For the methods and manners in the busy rush of life in the West vary entirely from those of India. Yet perhaps it will be of all the more interest for that, because it will bring into a newer light, things about which many have already heard.

It was while reforms of various kinds were being inaugurated in India that a child was born of poor Brâhmin parents on the eighteenth of February, 1836, in one of the remote villages of Bengal. The father and mother were very orthodox people. The life of a really orthodox Brahmin is one of continuous renunciation. Very few things can he do; and over and beyond them the orthodox Brahmin must not occupy himself with any secular business. At the same time he must not receive gifts from everybody. You may imagine how rigorous that life becomes. You have heard of the Brahmins and their priestcraft many times, but very few of you have ever stopped to ask what makes this wonderful band of men the rulers of their fellows. They are the poorest of all the classes in the country; and the secret of their power lies in their renunciation. They never covet wealth. Theirs is the poorest priesthood in the world, and therefore the most powerful. Even in this poverty, a Brahmin's wife will never allow a poor man to pass through the village without giving him something to eat. That is considered the highest duty of the mother in India; and because she is the mother it is her duty to be served last; she must see that everyone is served before her turn comes. That is why the mother is regarded as God in India. This particular woman, the mother of our subject, was the very type of a Hindu mother. The higher the caste, the greater the restrictions. The lowest caste people can eat and drink anything they like. But as men rise in the social scale, more and more restrictions come; and when they reach the highest caste, the Brahmin, the hereditary priesthood of India, their lives, as I have said, are very much circumscribed. Compared to Western manners, their lives are of continuous asceticism. The Hindus are perhaps the most exclusive nation in the world. They have the same great steadiness as the English, but much more amplified. When they get hold of an idea they carry it out to its very conclusion, and they, keep hold of it generation after generation until they make something out of it. Once give them an idea, and it is not easy to take it back; but it is hard to make them grasp a new idea.

The orthodox Hindus, therefore, are very exclusive, living entirely within their own horizon of thought and feeling. Their lives are laid down in our old books in every little detail, and the least detail is grasped with almost adamantine firmness by them. They would starve rather than eat a meal cooked by the hands of a man not belonging to their own small section of caste. But withal, they have intensity and tremendous earnestness. That force of intense faith and religious life occurs often among the orthodox Hindus, because their very orthodoxy comes from a tremendous conviction that it is right. We may not all think that what they hold on to with such perseverance is right; but to them it is. Now, it is written in our books that a man should always be charitable even to the extreme. If a man starves himself to death to help another man, to save that man's life, it is all right; it is even held that a man ought to do that. And it is expected of a Brahmin to carry this idea out to the very extreme. Those who are acquainted with the literature of India will remember a beautiful old story about this extreme charity, how a whole family, as related in the Mahâbhârata, starved themselves to death and gave their last meal to a beggar. This is not an exaggeration, for such things still happen. The character of the father and the mother of my Master was very much like that. Very poor they were, and yet many a time the mother would starve herself a whole day to help a poor man. Of them this child was born; and he was a peculiar child from very boyhood. He remembered his past from his birth and was conscious for what purpose he came into the world, and every power was devoted to the fulfilment of that purpose.

While he was quite young, his father died; and the boy was sent to school. A Brahmin's boy must go to school; the caste restricts him to a learned profession only. The old system of education in India, still prevalent in many parts of the country, especially in connection with Sannyasins, is very different from the modern system. The students had not to pay. It was thought that knowledge is so sacred that no man ought to sell it. Knowledge must be given freely and without any price. The teachers used to take students without charge, and not only so, most of them gave their students food and clothes. To support these teachers the wealthy families on certain occasions, such as a marriage festival, or at the ceremonies for the dead, made gifts to them. They were considered the first and foremost claimants to certain gifts; and they in their turn had to maintain their students. So whenever there is a marriage, especially in a rich family, these professors are invited, and they attend and discuss various subjects. This boy went to one of these gatherings of professors, and the professors were discussing various topics, such as logic or astronomy, subjects much beyond his age. The boy was peculiar, as I have said, and he gathered this moral out of it: "This is the outcome of all their knowledge. Why are they fighting so hard? It is simply for money; the man who can show the highest learning here will get the best pair of cloth, and that is all these people are struggling for. I will not go to school any more." And he did not; that was the end of his going to school. But this boy had an elder brother, a learned professor, who took him to Calcutta, however, to study with him. After a short time the boy became fully convinced that the aim of all secular learning was mere material advancement, and nothing more, and he resolved to give up study and devote himself solely to the pursuit of spiritual knowledge. The father being dead, the family was very poor; and this boy had to make his own living. He went to a place near Calcutta and became a temple priest. To become a temple priest is thought very degrading to a Brahmin. Our temples are not churches in your sense of the word, they are not places for public worship; for, properly speaking, there is no such thing as public worship in India. Temples are erected mostly by rich persons as a meritorious religious act.

If a man has much property, he wants to build a temple. In that he puts a symbol or an image of an Incarnation of God, and dedicates it to worship in the name of God. The worship is akin to that which is conducted in Roman Catholic churches, very much like the mass, reading certain sentences from the sacred books, waving a light before the image, and treating the image in every respect as we treat a great man. This is all that is done in the temple. The man who goes to a temple is not considered thereby a better man than he who never goes. More properly, the latter is considered the more religious man, for religion in India is to each man his own private affair. In the house of every man there is either a little chapel, or a room set apart, and there he goes morning and evening, sits down in a corner, and there does his worship. And this worship is entirely mental, for another man does not hear or know what he is doing. He sees him only sitting there, and perhaps moving his fingers in a peculiar fashion, or closing his nostrils and breathing in a peculiar manner. Beyond that, he does not know what his brother is doing; even his wife, perhaps, will not know. Thus, all worship is conducted in the privacy of his own home. Those who cannot afford to have a chapel go to the banks of a river, or a lake, or the sea if they live at the seaside, but people sometimes go to worship in a temple by making salutation to the image. There their duty to the temple ends. Therefore, you see, it has been held from the most ancient times in our country, legislated upon by Manu, that it is a degenerating occupation to become a temple priest. Some of the books say it is so degrading as to make a Brahmin worthy of reproach. Just as with education, but in a far more intense sense with religion, there is the other idea behind it that the temple priests who take fees for their work are making merchandise of sacred things. So you may imagine the feelings of that boy when he was forced through poverty to take up the only occupation open to him, that of a temple priest.

There have been various poets in Bengal whose songs have passed down to the people; they are sung in the streets of Calcutta and in every village. Most of these are religious songs, and their one central idea, which is perhaps peculiar to the religions of India, is the idea of realisation. There is not a book in India on religion which does not breathe this idea. Man must realise God, feel God, see God, talk to God. That is religion. The Indian atmosphere is full of stories of saintly persons having visions of God. Such doctrines form the basis of their religion; and all these ancient books and scriptures are the writings of persons who came into direct contact with spiritual facts. These books were not written for the intellect, nor can any reasoning understand them, because they were written by men who saw the things of which they wrote, and they can be understood only by men who have raised themselves to the same height. They say there is such a thing as realisation even in this life, and it is open to everyone, and religion begins with the opening of this faculty, if I may call it so. This is the central idea in all religions, and this is why we may find one man with the most finished oratorical powers, or the most convincing logic, preaching the highest doctrines and yet unable to get people to listen to him, while we may find another, a poor man, who scarcely can speak the language of his own motherland, yet half the nation worships him in his own lifetime as God. When in India the idea somehow or other gets abroad that a man has raised himself to that state of realisation, that religion is no more a matter of conjecture to him, that he is no more groping in the dark in such momentous questions as religion, the immortality of the soul, and God, people come from all quarters to see him and gradually they begin to worship him.

In the temple was an image of the "Blissful Mother". This boy had to conduct the worship morning and evening, and by degrees this one idea filled his mind: "Is there anything behind this images? Is it true that there is a Mother of Bliss in the universe? Is it true that She lives and guides the universe, or is it all a dream? Is there any reality in religion?"

This scepticism comes to the Hindu child. It is the scepticism of our country: Is this that we are doing real? And theories will not satisfy us, although there are ready at hand almost all the theories that have ever been made with regard to God and soul. Neither books nor theories can satisfy us, the one idea that gets hold of thousands of our people is this idea of realisation. Is it true that there is a God? If it be true, can I see Him? Can I realise the truth? The Western mind may think all this very impracticable, but to us it is intensely practical. For this their lives. You have just heard how from the earliest times there have been persons who have given up all comforts and luxuries to live in caves, and hundreds have given up their homes to weep bitter tears of misery, on the banks of sacred rivers, in order to realise this idea — not to know in the ordinary sense of the word, not intellectual understanding, not a mere rationalistic comprehension of the real thing, not mere groping in the dark, but intense realisation, much more real than this world is to our senses. That is the idea. I do not advance any proposition as to that just now, but that is the one fact that is impressed upon them. Thousands will be killed, other thousands will be ready. So upon this one idea the whole nation for thousands of years have been denying and sacrificing themselves. For this idea thousands of Hindus every year give up their homes, and many of them die through the hardships they have to undergo. To the Western mind this must seem most visionary, and I can see the reason for this point of view. But though I have resided in the West, I still think this idea the most practical thing in life.

Every moment I think of anything else is so much loss to me — even the marvels of earthly sciences; everything is vain if it takes me away from that thought. Life is but momentary, whether you have the knowledge of an angel or the ignorance of an animal. Life is but momentary, whether you have the poverty of the poorest man in rags or the wealth of the richest living person. Life is but momentary, whether you are a downtrodden man living in one of the big streets of the big cities of the West or a crowned Emperor ruling over millions. Life is but momentary, whether you have the best of health or the worst. Life is but momentary, whether you have the most poetical temperament or the most cruel. There is but one solution of life, says the Hindu, and that solution is what they call God and religion. If these be true, life becomes explained, life becomes bearable, becomes enjoyable. Otherwise, life is but a useless burden. That is our idea, but no amount of reasoning can demonstrate it; it can only make it probable, and there it rests. The highest demonstration of reasoning that we have in any branch of knowledge can only make a fact probable, and nothing further. The most demonstrable facts of physical science are only probabilities, not facts yet. Facts are only in the senses. Facts have to be perceived, and we have to perceive religion to demonstrate it to ourselves. We have to sense God to be convinced that there is a God. We must sense the facts of religion to know that they are facts. Nothing else, and no amount of reasoning, but our own perception can make these things real to us, can make my belief firm as a rock. That is my idea, and that is the Indian idea.

This idea took possession of the boy and his whole life became concentrated upon that. Day after day he would weep and say, "Mother, is it true that Thou existest, or is it all poetry? Is the Blissful Mother an imagination of poets and misguided people, or is there such a Reality?" We have seen that of books, of education in our sense of the word, he had none, and so much the more natural, so much the more healthy, was his mind, so much the purer his thoughts, undiluted by drinking in the thoughts of others. Because he did not go to the university, therefore he thought for himself. Because we have spent half our lives in the university we are filled with a collection of other people's thoughts. Well has Prof. Max Müller said in the article I have just referred to that this was a clean, original man; and the secret of that originality was that he was not brought up within the precincts of a university. However, this thought — whether God can be seen — which was uppermost in his mind gained in strength every day until he could think of nothing else. He could no more conduct the worship properly, could no more attend to the various details in all their minuteness. Often he would forget to place the food-offering before the image, sometimes he would forget to wave the light; at other times he would wave it for hours, and forget everything else.

And that one idea was in his mind every day: "Is it true that Thou existest, O Mother? Why cost Thou not speak? Art Thou dead?" Perhaps some of us here will remember that there are moments in our lives when, tired of all these ratiocinations of dull and dead logic, tired of plodding through books — which after all teach us nothing, become nothing but a sort of intellectual opium-eating — we must have it at stated times or we die — tired with all this, the heart of our hearts sends out a wail: "Is there no one in this universe who can show me the light? If Thou art, show the light unto me. Why dost Thou not speak? Why dost Thou make Thyself so scarce, why send so many Messengers and not Thyself come to me? In this world of fights and factions whom am I to follow and believe? If Thou art the God of every man and woman alike, why comest Thou not to speak to Thy child and see if he is not ready?" Well, to us all come such thoughts in moments of great depression; but such are the temptations surrounding us, that the next moment we forget. For the moment it seemed that the doors of the heavens were going to be opened, for the moment it seemed as if we were going to plunge into the light effulgent; but the animal man again shakes off all these angelic visions. Down we go, animal man once more eating and drinking and dying, and dying and drinking and eating again and again. But there are exceptional minds which are not turned away so easily, which once attracted can never be turned back, whatever may be the temptation in the way, which want to see the Truth knowing that life must go. They say, let it go in a noble conquest, and what conquest is nobler than the conquest of the lower man, than this solution of the problem of life and death, of good and evil?

At last it became impossible for him to serve in the temple. He left it and entered into a little wood that was near and lived there. About this part of his life, he told me many times that he could not tell when the sun rose or set, or how he lived. He lost all thought of himself and forgot to eat. During this period he was lovingly watched over by a relative who put into his mouth food which he mechanically swallowed.

Days and nights thus passed with the boy. When a whole day would pass, towards the evening when the peal of bells in the temples, and the voices singing, would reach the wood, it would make the boy very sad, and he would cry, "Another day is gone in vain, Mother, and Thou hast not come. Another day of this short life has gone, and I have not known the Truth." In the agony of his soul, sometimes he would rub his face against the ground and weep, and this one prayer burst forth: "Do Thou manifest Thyself in me, Thou Mother of the universe! See that I need Thee and nothing else!" Verily, he wanted to be true to his own ideal. He had heard that the Mother never came until everything had been given up for Her. He had heard that the Mother wanted to come to everyone, but they would not have Her, that people wanted all sorts of foolish little idols to pray to, that they wanted their own enjoyments, and not the Mother, and that the moment they really wanted Her with their whole soul, and nothing else, that moment She would come. So he began to break himself into that idea; he wanted to be exact, even on the plane of matter. He threw away all the little property he had, and took a vow that he would never touch money, and this one idea, "I will not touch money", became a part of him. It may appear to be something occult, but even in after-life when he was sleeping, if I touched him with a piece of money his hand would become bent, and his whole body would become, as it were, paralysed. The other idea that came into his mind was that lust was the other enemy. Man is a soul, and soul is sexless, neither man nor woman. The idea of sex and the idea of money were the two things, he thought, that prevented him from seeing the Mother. This whole universe is the manifestation of the Mother, and She lives in every woman's body. "Every woman represents the Mother; how can I think of woman in mere sex relation?" That was the idea: Every woman was his Mother, he must bring himself to the state when he would see nothing but Mother in every woman. And he carried it out in his life.

This is the tremendous thirst that seizes the human heart. Later on, this very man said to me, "My child, suppose there is a bag of gold in one room, and a robber in the next room; do you think that the robber can sleep? He cannot. His mind will be always thinking how to get into that room and obtain possession of that gold. Do you think then that a man, firmly persuaded that there is a Reality behind all these appearances, that there is a God, that there is One who never dies, One who is infinite bliss, a bliss compared with which these pleasures of the senses are simply playthings, can rest contented without struggling to attain It? Can he cease his efforts for a moment? No. He will become mad with longing." This divine madness seized the boy. At that time he had no teacher, nobody to tell him anything, and everyone thought that he was out of his mind. This is the ordinary condition of things. If a man throws aside the vanities of the world, we hear him called mad. But such men are the salt of the earth. Out of such madness have come the powers that have moved this world of ours, and out of such madness alone will come the powers of the future that are going to move the world.

So days, weeks, months passed in continuous struggle of the soul to arrive at truth. The boy began to see visions, to see wonderful things; the secrets of his nature were beginning to open to him. Veil after veil was, as it were, being taken off. Mother Herself became the teacher and initiated the boy into the truths he sought. At this time there came to this place a woman of beautiful appearance, learned beyond compare. Later on, this saint used to say about her that she was not learned, but was the embodiment of learning; she was learning itself, in human form. There, too, you find the peculiarity of the Indian nation. In the midst of the ignorance in which the average Hindu woman lives, in the midst of what is called in Western countries her lack of freedom, there could arise a woman of supreme spirituality. She was a Sannyâsini; for women also give up the world, throw away their property, do not marry, and devote themselves to the worship of the Lord. She came; and when she heard of this boy in the grove, she offered to go and see him; and hers was the first help he received. At once she recognised what his trouble was, and she said to him. "My son blessed is the man upon whom such madness comes. The whole of this universe is mad — some for wealth, some for pleasure, some for fame, some for a hundred other things. They are mad for gold, or husbands, or wives, for little trifles, mad to tyrannise over somebody, mad to become rich, mad for every foolish thing except God. And they can understand only their own madness. When another man is mad after gold, they have fellow-feeling and sympathy for him, and they say he is the right man, as lunatics think that lunatics alone are sane. But if a man is mad after the Beloved, after the Lord, how can they understand? They think he has gone crazy; and they say, 'Have nothing to do with him.' That is why they call you mad; but yours is the right kind of madness. Blessed is the man who is mad after God. Such men are very few." This woman remained near the boy for years, taught him the forms of the religions of India, initiated him into the different practices of Yoga, and, as it were, guided and brought into harmony this tremendous river of spirituality.

Later, there came to the same grove a Sannyasin, one of the begging friars of India, a learned man, a philosopher. He was a peculiar man, he was an idealist. He did not believe that this world existed in reality; and to demonstrate that, he would never go under a roof, he would always live out of doors, in storm and sunshine alike. This man began to teach the boy the philosophy of the Vedas; and he found very soon, to his astonishment, that the pupil was in some respects wiser than the master. He spent several months with the boy, after which he initiated him into the order of Sannyasins, and took his departure.

When as a temple priest his extraordinary worship made people think him deranged in his head, his relatives took him home and married him to a little girl, thinking that that would turn his thoughts and restore the balance of his mind. But he came back and, as we have seen, merged deeper in his madness. Sometimes, in our country, boys are married as children and have no voice in the matter; their parents marry them. Of course such a marriage is little more than a betrothal. When they are married they still continue to live with their parents, and the real marriage takes place when the wife grows older, Then it is customary for the husband to go and bring his bride to his own home. In this case, however, the husband had entirely forgotten that he had a wife. In her far off home the girl had heard that her husband had become a religious enthusiast, and that he was even considered insane by many. She resolved to learn the truth for herself, so she set out and walked to the place where her husband was. When at last she stood in her husband's presence, he at once admitted her right to his life, although in India any person, man or woman, who embraces a religious life, is thereby freed from all other obligations. The young man fell at the feet of his wife and said, "As for me, the Mother has shown me that She resides in every woman, and so I have learnt to look upon every woman as Mother. That is the one idea I can have about you; but if you wish to drag me into the world, as I have been married to you, I am at your service."

The maiden was a pure and noble soul and was able to understand her husband's aspirations and sympathise with them. She quickly told him that she had no wish to drag him down to a life of worldliness; but that all she desired was to remain near him, to serve him, and to learn of him. She became one of his most devoted disciples, always revering him as a divine being. Thus through his wife's consent the last barrier was removed, and he was free to lead the life he had chosen.

The next desire that seized upon the soul of this man as to know the truth about the various religions. Up to that time he had not known any religion but his own. He wanted to understand what other religions were like. So he sought teachers of other religions. By teachers you must always remember what we mean in India, not a bookworm, but a man of realisation, one who knows truth a; first hand and not through an intermediary. He found a Mohammedan saint and placed himself under him; he underwent the disciplines prescribed by him, and to his astonishment found that when faithfully carried out, these devotional methods led him to the same goal he had already attained. He gathered similar experience from following the true religion of Jesus the Christ. He went to all the sects he could find, and whatever he took up he went into with his whole heart. He did exactly as he was told, and in every instance he arrived at the same result. Thus from actual experience, he came to know that the goal of every religion is the same, that each is trying to teach the same thing, the difference being largely in method and still more in language. At the core, all sects and all religions have the same aim; and they were only quarrelling for their own selfish purposes — they were not anxious about the truth, but about "my name" and "your name". Two of them preached the same truth, but one of them said, "That cannot be true, because I have not put upon it the seal of my name. Therefore do not listen to him." And the other man said, "Do not hear him, although he is preaching very much the same thing, yet it is not true because he does not preach it in my name."

That is what my Master found, and he then set about to learn humility, because he had found that the one idea in all religions is, "not me, but Thou", and he who says, "not me", the Lord fills his heart. The less of this little "I" the more of God there is in him. That he found to be the truth in every religion in the world, and he set himself to accomplish this. As I have told you, whenever he wanted to do anything he never confined himself to fine theories, but would enter into the practice immediately; We see many persons talking the most wonderfully fine things about charity and about equality and the rights of other people and all that, but it is only in theory. I was so fortunate as to find one who was able to carry theory into practice. He had the most wonderful faculty of carrying everything into practice which he thought was right.

Now, there was a family of Pariahs living near the place. The Pariahs number several millions in the whole of India and are a sect of people so low that some of our books say that if a Brahmin coming out from his house sees the face of a Pariah, he has to fast that day and recite certain prayers before he becomes holy again. In some Hindu cities when a Pariah enters, he has to put a crow's feather on his head as a sign that he is a Pariah, and he has to cry aloud, "Save yourselves, the Pariah is passing through the street", and you will find people flying off from him as if by magic, because if they touch him by chance, they will have to change their clothes, bathe, and do other things. And the Pariah for thousands of years has believed that it is perfectly right; that his touch will make everybody unholy. Now my Master would go to a Pariah and ask to be allowed to clean his house. The business of the Pariah is to clean the streets of the cities and to keep houses clean. He cannot enter the house by the front door; by the back door he enters; and as soon as he has gone, the whole place over which he has passed is sprinkled with and made holy by a little Gangâ water. By birth the Brahmin stands for holiness, and the Pariah for the very reverse. And this Brahmin asked to be allowed to do the menial services in the house of the Pariah. The Pariah of course could not allow that, for they all think that if they allow a Brahmin to do such menial work it will be an awful sin, and they will become extinct. The Pariah would not permit it; so in the dead of night, when all were sleeping, Ramakrishna would enter the house. He had long hair, and with his hair he would wipe the place, saying, "Oh, my Mother, make me the servant of the Pariah, make me feel that I am even lower than the Pariah." "They worship Me best who worship My worshippers. These are all My children and your privilege is to serve them" — is the teaching of Hindu scriptures.

There were various other preparations which would take a long time to relate, and I want to give you just a sketch of his life. For years he thus educated himself. One of the Sâdhanâs was to root out the sex idea. Soul has no sex, it is neither male nor female. It is only in the body that sex exists, and the man who desires to reach the spirit cannot at the same time hold to sex distinctions. Having been born in a masculine body, this man wanted to bring the feminine idea into everything. He began to think that he was a woman, he dressed like a woman, spoke like a woman, gave up the occupations of men, and lived in the household among the women of a good family, until, after years of this discipline, his mind became changed, and he entirely forgot the idea of sex; thus the whole view of life became changed to him.

We hear in the West about worshipping woman, but this is usually for her youth and beauty. This man meant by worshipping woman, that to him every woman's face was that of the Blissful Mother, and nothing but that. I myself have seen this man standing before those women whom society would not touch, and falling at their feet bathed in tears, saying, "Mother, in one form Thou art in the street, and in another form Thou art the universe. I salute Thee, Mother, I salute Thee." Think of the blessedness of that life from which all carnality has vanished, which can look upon every woman with that love and reverence when every woman's face becomes transfigured, and only the face of the Divine Mother, the Blissful One, the Protectress of the human race, shines upon it! That is what we want. Do you mean to say that the divinity back of a woman can ever be cheated? It never was and never will be, It always asserts itself. Unfailingly it detects fraud, it detects hypocrisy, unerringly it feels the warmth of truth, the light of spirituality, the holiness of purity. Such purity is absolutely necessary if real spirituality is to be attained.

This rigorous, unsullied purity came into the life of that man. All the struggles which we have in our lives were past for him. His hard-earned jewels of spirituality, for which he had given three-quarters of his life, were now ready to be given to humanity, and then began his mission. His teaching and preaching were peculiar. In our country a teacher is a most highly venerated person, he is regarded as God Himself. We have not even the same respect for our father and mother. Father and mother give us our body, but the teacher shows us the way to salvation. We are his children, we are born in the spiritual line of the teacher. All Hindus come to pay respect to an extraordinary teacher, they crowd around him. And here was such a teacher, but the teacher had no thought whether he was to be respected or not, he had not the least idea that he was a great teacher, he thought that it was Mother who was doing everything and not he. He always said, "If any good comes from my lips, It is the Mother who speaks; what have I to do with It?" That was his one idea about his work, and to the day of his death he never gave it up. This man sought no one. His principle was, first form character, first earn spirituality and results will come of themselves. His favourite illustration was, "When the lotus opens, the bees come of their own accord to seek the honey; so let the lotus of your character be full-blown, and the results will follow." This is a great lesson to learn.

My Master taught me this lesson hundreds of times, yet I often forget it. Few understand the power of thought. If a man goes into a cave, shuts himself in, and thinks one really great thought and dies, that thought will penetrate the walls of that cave, vibrate through space, and at last permeate the whole human race. Such is the power of thought; be in no hurry therefore to give your thoughts to others. First have something to give. He alone teaches who has something to give, for teaching is not talking, teaching is not imparting doctrines, it is communicating. Spirituality can be communicated just as really as I can give you a flower. This is true in the most literal sense. This idea is very old in India and finds illustration in the West in the "theory, in the belief, of apostolic succession. Therefore first make character — that is the highest duty you can perform. Know Truth for yourself, and there will be many to whom you can teach it after wards; they will all come. This was the attitude of nay Master. He criticised no one. For years I lived with that man, but never did I hear those lips utter one word of condemnation for any sect. He had the same sympathy for all sects; he had found the harmony between them. A man may be intellectual, or devotional, or mystic, or active; the various religions represent one or the other of these types. Yet it is possible to combine all the four in one man, and this is what future humanity is going to do. That was his idea. He condemned no one, but saw the good in all.

People came by thousands to see and hear this wonderful man who spoke in a *patois* every word of which was forceful and instinct with light. For it is not what is spoken, much less the language in which it is spoken, but it is the personality of the speaker which dwells in everything he says that carries weight. Every one of us feels this at times. We hear most splendid orations, most wonderfully reasoned-out discourses, and we go home and forget them all. At other times we hear a few words in the simplest language, and they enter into our lives, become part and parcel of ourselves and produce lasting results. The words of a man who can put his personality into them take effect, but he must have tremendous personality. All teaching implies giving and taking, the teacher gives and the taught receives, but the one must have something to give, and the other must be open to receive.

This man came to live near Calcutta, the capital of India, the most important university town in our country which was sending out sceptics and materialists by the hundreds every year. Yet many of these university men — sceptics and agnostics — used to come and listen to him. I heard of this man, and I went to hear him. He looked just like an ordinary man, with nothing remarkable about him. He used the most simple language, and I thought "Can this man be a great teacher?" — crept near to him and asked him the question which I had been asking others all my life: "Do you believe in God, Sir?" "Yes," he replied. "Can you prove it, Sir?" "Yes." "How?" "Because I see Him just as I see you here, only in a much intenser sense." That impressed me at once. For the first time I found a man who dared to say that he saw God that religion was a reality to be felt, to be sensed in an infinitely more intense way than we can sense the world. I began to go to that man, day after day, and I actually saw that religion could be given. One touch, one glance, can change a whole life. I have read about Buddha and Christ and Mohammed, about all those different luminaries of ancient times, how they would stand up and say, "Be thou whole", and the man became whole. I now found it to be true, and when I myself saw this man, all scepticism was brushed aside. It could be done; and my Master used to say, "Religion can be given and taken more tangibly, more really than anything else in the world." Be therefore spiritual first; have something to give and then stand before the world and give it. Religion is not talk, or doctrines, or theories; nor is it sectarianism. Religion cannot live in sects and societies. It is the relation between the soul and God; how can it be made into a society? It would then degenerate into business, and wherever there are business and business principles in religion, spirituality dies. Religion does not consist in erecting temples, or building churches, or attending public worship. It is not to be found in books, or in words, or in lectures, or in organisations. Religion consists in realisation. As a fact, we all know that nothing will satisfy us until we know the truth for ourselves. However we may argue, however much we may hear, but one thing will satisfy us, and that is our own realisation; and such an experience is possible for every one of us if we will only try. The first ideal of this attempt to realise religion is that of renunciation. As far as we can, we must give up. Darkness and light, enjoyment of the world and enjoyment of God will never go together. "Ye cannot serve God and Mammon." Let people try it if they will, and I have seen millions in every country who have tried; but after all, it comes to nothing. If one word remains true in the saying, it is, give up every thing for the sake of the Lord. This is a hard and long task, but you can begin it here and now. Bit by bit we must go towards it.

The second idea that I learnt from my Master, and which is perhaps the most vital, is the wonderful truth that the religions of the world are not contradictory or antagonistic. They are but various phases of one eternal religion. That one eternal religion is applied to different planes of existence, is applied to the opinions of various minds and various races. There never was my religion or yours, my national religion or your national religion; there never existed many religions, there is only the one. One infinite religion existed all through eternity and will ever exist, and this religion is expressing itself in various countries in various ways. Therefore we must respect all religions and we must try to accept them all as far as we can. Religions manifest themselves not only according to race and geographical position, but according to individual powers. In one man religion is manifesting itself as intense activity, as work. In another it is manifesting itself as intense devotion, in yet another, as mysticism, in others as philosophy, and so forth. It is wrong when we say to others, "Your methods are not right." Perhaps a man, whose nature is that of love, thinks that the man who does good to others is not on the right road to religion, because it is not his own way, and is therefore wrong. If the philosopher thinks, "Oh, the poor ignorant people, what do they know about a God of Love, and loving Him? They do not know what they mean," he is wrong, because they may be right and he also.

To learn this central secret that the truth may be one and yet many at the same time, that we may have different visions of the same truth from different standpoints, is exactly what must be done. Then, instead of antagonism to anyone, we shall have infinite sympathy with all. Knowing that as long as there are different natures born in this world, the same religious truth will require different adaptations, we shall understand that we are bound to have forbearance with each other. Just as nature is unity in variety — an infinite variation in the phenomenal — as in and through all these variations of the phenomenal runs the Infinite, the Unchangeable, the Absolute Unity, so it is with every man; the microcosm is but a miniature repetition of the macrocosm; in spite of all these variations, in and through them all runs this eternal harmony, and we have to recognise this. This idea, above all other ideas, I find to be the crying necessity of the day. Coming from a country which is a hotbed of religious sects — and to which, through its good fortune or ill fortune, everyone who has a religious idea wants to send an advance-guard — I have been acquainted from my childhood with the various sects of the world. Even the Mormons come to preach in India. Welcome them all! That is the soil on which to preach religion. There it takes root more than in any other country. If you come and teach politics to the Hindus, they do not understand; but if you come to preach religion, however curious it may be, you will have hundreds and thousands of followers in no time, and you have every chance of becoming a living God in your lifetime. I am glad it is so, it is the one thing we want in India.

The sects among the Hindus are various, a great many in number, and some of them apparently hopelessly contradictory. Yet they all tell you they are but different manifestations of religion. "As different rivers, taking their start from different mountains, running crooked or straight, all come and mingle their waters in the ocean, so the different sects, with their different points of vied, at last all come unto Thee." This is not a theory, it has to be recognised, but not in that patronising way which we see with some people: "Oh yes, there are some very good things in it. These are what we call the ethnical religions. These ethnical religions have some good in them." Some even have the most wonderfully liberal idea that other religions are all little bits of a prehistoric evolution, but "ours is the fulfilment of things". One man says, because his is the oldest religion, it is the best: another makes the same claim, because his is the latest.

We have to recognise that each one of them has the same saving power as the other. What you have heard about their difference, whether in the temple or in the church, is a mass of superstition. The same God answers all; and it is not you, or I, or any body of men that is responsible for the safety and salvation of the least little bit of the soul; the same Almighty God is responsible for all. I do not understand how people declare themselves to be believers in God, and at the same time think that God has handed over to a little body of men all truth, and that they are the guardians of the rest of humanity. How can you call that religion? Religion is realisation; but mere talk — mere trying to believe, mere groping in darkness, mere parroting the words of ancestors and thinking it is religion, mere making a political something out of the truths of religion — is not religion at all. In every sect — even among the Mohammedans whom we always regard as the most exclusive — even among them we find that wherever there was a man trying to realise religion, from his lips have come the fiery words: "Thou art the Lord of all, Thou art in the heart of all, Thou art the guide of all, Thou art the Teacher of all, and Thou caress infinitely more for the land of Thy children than we can ever do." Do not try to disturb the faith of any man. If you can, give him something better; if you can, get hold of a man where he stands and give him a push upwards; do so, but do not destroy what he has. The only true teacher is he who can convert himself, as it were, into a thousand persons at a moment's notice. The only true teacher is he who can immediately come down to the level of the student, and transfer his soul to the student's soul and see through the student's eyes and hear through his ears and understand through his mind. Such a teacher can really teach and none else. All these negative, breaking-down, destructive teachers that are in the world can never do any good.

In the presence of my Master I found out that man could be perfect, even in this body. Those lips never cursed anyone, never even criticised anyone. Those eyes were beyond the possibility of seeing evil, that mind had lost the power of thinking evil. He saw nothing but good. That tremendous purity, that tremendous renunciation is the one secret of spirituality. "Neither through wealth, nor through progeny, but through renunciation alone, is immortality to be reached", say the Vedas. "Sell all that thou hast and give to the poor, and follow me", says the Christ. So all great saints and Prophets have expressed it, and have carried it out in their lives. How can great spirituality come without that renunciation? Renunciation is the background of all religious thought wherever it be, and you will always find that as this idea of renunciation lessens, the more will the senses creep into the field of religion, and spirituality will decrease in the same ratio.

That man was the embodiment of renunciation. In our country it is necessary for a man who becomes a Sannyasin to give up all worldly wealth and position, and this my Master carried out literally. There were many who would have felt themselves blest if he would only have accepted a present from their hands, who would gladly have given him thousands of rupees if he would have taken them, but these were the only men from whom he would turn away. He was a triumphant example, a living realisation of the complete conquest of lust and of desire for money. He was beyond all ideas of either, and such men are necessary for this century. Such renunciation is necessary in these days when men have begun to think that they cannot live a month without what they call their "necessities", and which they are increasing out of all proportion. It is necessary in a time like this that a man should arise to demonstrate to the sceptics of the world that there yet breathes a man who does not care a straw for all the gold or all the fame that is in the universe. Yet there are such men.

The other idea of his life was intense love for others. The first part of my Master's life was spent in acquiring spirituality, and the remaining years in distributing it. People in our country have not the same customs as you have in visiting a religious teacher or a Sannyasin. Somebody would come to ask him about something, some perhaps would come hundreds of miles, walking all the way, just to ask one question, to hear one word from him, "Tell me one word for my salvation." That is the way they come. They come in numbers, unceremoniously, to the place where he is mostly to be found; they may find him under a tree and question him; and before one set of people has gone, others have arrived. So if a man is greatly revered, he will sometimes have no rest day or night. He will have to talk constantly. For hours people will come pouring in, and this man will be teaching them.

So men came in crowds to hear him, and he would talk twenty hours in the twenty-four, and that not for one day, but for months and months until at last the body broke down under the pressure of this tremendous strain. His intense love for mankind would not let him refuse to help even the humblest of the thousands who sought his aid. Gradually, there developed a vital throat disorder and yet he could not be persuaded to refrain from these exertions. As soon as he heard that people were asking to see him, he would insist upon having them admitted and would answer all their questions. When expostulated with, he replied, "I do not care. I will give up twenty thousand such bodies to help one man. It is glorious to help even one man." There was no rest for him. Once a man asked him, "Sir, you are a great Yogi. Why do you not put your mind a little on your body and cure your disease? "At first he did not answer, but when the question had been repeated, he gently said, "My friend, I thought you were a sage, but you talk like other men of the world. This mind has been given to the Lord. Do you mean to say that I should take it back and put it upon the body which is but a mere cage of the soul?"

So he went on preaching to the people, and the news spread that his body was about to pass away, and the people began to flock to him in greater crowds than ever. You cannot imagine the way they come to these great religious teachers in India, how they crowd round them and make gods of them while they are yet living. Thousands wait simply to touch the hem of their garments. It is through this appreciation of spirituality in others that spirituality is produced. Whatever man wants and appreciates, he will get; and it is the same with nations. If you go to India and deliver a political lecture, however grand it may be, you will scarcely find people to listen to you but just go and teach religion, *live* it, not merely talk it, and hundreds will crowd just to look at you, to touch your feet. When the people heard that this holy man was likely to go from them soon, they began to come round him more than ever, and my Master went on teaching them without the least regard for his health. We could not prevent this. Many of the people came from long distances, and he would not rest until he had answered their questions. "While I can speak, I must teach them," he would say, and he was as good as his word. One day, he told us that he would lay down the body that day, and repeating the most sacred word of the Vedas he entered into Samâdhi and passed away.

His thoughts and his message were known to very few capable of giving them out. Among others, he left a few young boys who had renounced the world, and were ready to carry on his work. Attempts were made to crush them. But they stood firm, having the inspiration of that great life before them. Having had the contact of that blessed life for years, they stood their ground. These young men, living as Sannyasins, begged through the streets of the city where they were born, although some of them came from high families. At first they met with great antagonism, but they persevered and went on from day to day spreading all over India the message of that great man, until the whole country was filled with the ideas he had preached. This man, from a remote village of Bengal, without education, by the sheer force of his own determination, realised the truth and gave it to others, leaving only a few young boys to keep it alive.

Today the name of Shri Ramakrishna Paramahamsa is known all over India to its millions of people. Nay, the power of that man has spread beyond India; and if there has ever been a word of truth, a word of spirituality, that I have spoken anywhere in the world, I owe it to my Master; only the mistakes are mine.

This is the message of Shri Ramakrishna to the modern world: "Do not care for doctrines, do not care for dogmas, or sects, or churches, or temples; they count for little compared with the essence of existence in each man which is spirituality; and the more this is developed in a man, the more powerful is he for good. Earn that first, acquire that, and criticise no one, for all doctrines and creeds have some good in them. Show by your lives that religion does not mean words, or names, or sects, but that it means spiritual realisation. Only those can understand who have felt. Only those who have attained to spirituality can communicate it to others, can be great teachers of mankind. They alone are the powers of light."

The more such men are produced in a country, the more that country will be raised; and that country where such men absolutely do not exist is simply doomed nothing can save it. Therefore my Master's message to mankind is: "Be spiritual and realise truth for Yourself." He would have you give up for the sake of your fellow-beings. He would have you cease talking about love for your brother, and set to work to prove your words. The time has come for renunciation, for realisation, and then you will see the harmony in all the religions of the world. You will know that there is no need of any quarrel. And then only will you be ready to help humanity. To proclaim and make clear the fundamental unity underlying all religions was the mission of my Master. Other teachers have taught special religions which bear their names, but this great teacher of the nineteenth century made no claim for himself. He left every religion undisturbed because he had realised that in reality they are all part and parcel of the one eternal religion.

Indian Religious Thought

(Delivered under the auspices of tile Brooklyn Ethical Society, in the Art Gallery of tile Pouch Mansion, Clinton Avenue, Brooklyn, U.S.A.)

India, although only half the size of the United States, contains a population of over two hundred and ninety millions, and there are three religions which hold sway over them — the Mohammedan, the Buddhist (including the Jain), and the Hindu. The adherents of the first mentioned number about sixty millions, of the second about nine millions, while the last embrace nearly two hundred and six millions. The cardinal features of the Hindu religion are founded on the meditative and speculative philosophy and on the ethical teachings contained in the various books of the Vedas, which assert that the universe is infinite in space and eternal in duration. It never had a beginning, and it never will have an end. Innumerable have been the manifestations of the power of the spirit in the realm of matter, of the force of the Infinite in the domain of the finite; but the Infinite Spirit Itself is self-existent, eternal, and unchangeable. The passage of time makes no mark whatever on the dial of eternity. In its supersensuous region which cannot be comprehended at all by the human understanding, there is no past, and there is no future. The Vedas teach that the soul of man is immortal. The body is subject to the law of growth and decay, what grows must of necessity decay. But the in dwelling spirit is related to the infinite and eternal life; it never had a beginning and it never will have an end, One of the chief distinctions between the Hindu and the Christian religions is that the Christian religion teaches that each human soul had its beginning at its birth into this world, whereas the Hindu religion asserts that the spirit of man is an emanation of the Eternal Being, and had no more a beginning than God Himself. Innumerable have been and will be its manifestations in its passage from one personality to another, subject to the great law of spiritual evolution, until it reaches perfection, when there is no more change.

It has been often asked: If this be so, why is it we do not remember anything of our past lives? This is our explanation: Consciousness is the name of the surface only of the mental ocean, but within its depths are stored up all our experiences, both pleasant and painful. The desire of the human soul is to find out something that is stable. The mind and the body, in fact all the various phenomena of nature, are in a condition of incessant change. But the highest aspiration of our spirit is to find out something that does not change, that has reached a state of permanent perfection. And this is the aspiration of the human soul after the Infinite! The finer our moral and intellectual development, the stronger will become this aspiration after the Eternal that changes not.

The modern Buddhists teach that everything that cannot be known by the five senses is non-existent, and that it is a delusion to suppose that man is an independent entity. The idealists, on the contrary, claim that each individual is an independent entity, and the external world does not exist outside of his mental conception. But the sure solution of this problem is that nature is a mixture of independence and dependence, of reality and idealism. Our mind and bodies are dependent on the external world, and this dependence varies according to the nature of their relation to it; but the indwelling spirit is free, as God is free, and is able to direct in a greater or lesser degree, according to the state of their development, the movements of our minds and bodies.

Death is but a change of condition. We remain in the same universe, and are subject to the same laws as before. Those who have passed beyond and have attained high planes of development in beauty and wisdom are but the advance-guard of a universal army who are following after them. The spirit of the highest is related to the spirit of the lowest, and the germ of infinite perfection exists in all. We should cultivate the optimistic temperament, and endeavour to see the good that dwells in everything. If we sit down and lament over the imperfection of our bodies and minds, we profit nothing;

it is the heroic endeavour to subdue adverse circumstances that carries our spirit upwards. The object of life is to learn the laws of spiritual progress. Christians can learn from Hindus, and Hindus can learn from Christians. Each has made a contribution of value to the wisdom of the world.

Impress upon your children that true religion is positive and not negative, that it does not consist in merely refraining from evil, but in a persistent performance of noble decals. True religion comes not front the teaching of men or the reading of books; it is the awakening of the spirit within us, consequent upon pure and heroic action. Every child born into the world brings with it a certain accumulated experience from previous incarnations; and the impress of this experience is seen in the structure of its mind and body. But the feeling of independence which possesses us all shows there is something in us besides mind and body. The soul that reigns within is independent stud creates the desire for freedom. If we are not free, how can we hope to make the world better? We hold that human progress is the result of the action of the human spirit. What the world is, and what we ourselves are, are the fruits of the freedom of the spirit.

We believe in one God, the Father of us all, who is omnipresent and omnipotent, and who guides and preserves His children with infinite love. We believe in a Personal God as the Christians do, but we go further: we below that we are He! That His personality is manifested in us, that God is in us, and that we are in God We believe there is a germ of truth in all religions, and the Hindu bows down to them all; for in this world, truth is to be found not in subtraction but in addition. We would offer God a bouquet of the most beautiful flowers of all the diverse faiths. We must love God for love's sake, not for the hope of reward. We must do our duty for duty's sake not for the hope of reward. We must worship the beautiful for beauty's sake, not for the hope of reward. Thus in the purity of our hearts shall we see God. Sacrifices genuflexions, mumblings, and mutterings are not religion. They are only good if they stimulate us to the brave performance of beautiful and heroic deeds and lift our thoughts to the apprehension of the divine perfection

What good is it, if we acknowledge in our prayers that God is the Father of us all, and in our daily lives do not treat every man as our brother? Books are only made so that they may point the way to a higher life; but no good results unless the path is trodden with unflinching steps! Every human personality may be compared to a glass globe. There is the same pure white light — an emission of the divine Being — in the centre of each, but the glass being of different colours and thickness, the rays assume diverse aspects in the transmission. The equality and beauty of each central flame is the same, and the apparent inequality is only in the imperfection of the temporal instrument of its expression. As we rise higher and higher in the scale of being, the medium becomes more and more translucent.

The Basis For Psychic Or Spiritual Research

It was not often that Swami Vivekananda, while in the West, took part in debates. One such occasion in London when he did so was during the discussion of a lecture on, "Can Psychic Phenomena be proved from a Scientific Basis?" Referring first to a remark which he had heard in the course of this debate, not for the first time in the West, he said:

One point I want to remark upon. It is a mistaken statement that has been made to us that the Mohammedans do not believe that women have souls. I am very sorry to say it is an old mistake among Christian people, and they seem to like the mistake. That is a peculiarity in human nature, that people want to say something very bad about others whom they do not like. By the by, you know I am not a Mohammedan, but yet I have had opportunity for studying this religion, and there is not one word in the Koran which says that women have no souls, but in fact it says they have.

About the psychical things that have been the subject of discussion, I have very little to say here, for in the first place, the question is whether psychical subjects are capable of scientific demonstration. What do you mean by this demonstration? First of all, there will be the subjective and the objective side necessary. Taking chemistry and physics, with which we are so familiar, and of which we have read so much, is it true that everyone in this world is able to understand the demonstration even of the commonest subjects? Take any boor and show him one of your experiments. What will he understand of it? Nothing. It requires a good deal of previous training to be brought up to the point of understanding an experiment. Before that he cannot understand it at all. That is a area difficulty in the way. If scientific demonstration mean bringing down certain facts to a plane which is universe for all human beings, where all beings can understand it I deny that there can be any such scientific demonstration for any subject in the world. If it were so, all our universities and education would be in vain. Why are we educated if by birth we can understand everything scientific? Why so much study? It is of no use whatsoever. So, on the face of it, it is absurd if this be the meaning of scientific demonstration, the bringing down of intricate facts to the plane on which we are now. The next meaning should be the correct one, perhaps, that certain facts should be adduced as proving certain more intricate facts. There are certain more complicated intricate phenomena, which we explain by less intricate ones, and thus get, perhaps, nearer to them; in this way they are gradually brought down to the plane of our present ordinary consciousness. But even this is very complicated and very difficult, and means a training also, a tremendous amount of education. So an I have to say is that in order to have scientific explanation of psychical phenomena, we require not only perfect evidence on the side of the phenomena themselves, but a good deal of training on the part of those who want to see. All this being granted, we shall be in a position to say yea or nay, about the proof or disproof of any phenomena which are presented before us. But, before that, the most remarkable phenomena or the most oft-recorded phenomena that have happened in human society, in my opinion, would be very hard indeed to prove even in an offhand manner.

Next, as to those hasty explanations that religions are the outcome of dreams, those who have made a particular study of them would think of them but as mere guesses. We no reason to suppose that religions were the outcome of dreams as has been so easily explained. Then it would be very easy indeed to take even the agnostic's position, but unfortunately the matter cannot be explained so easily. There are many other wonderful phenomena happening, even at the present time, and these have all to be investigated, and not only have to be, but have been investigated all along. The blind man says there is no sun. That does not prove that there is no sun. These phenomena have been investigated years before. Whole races of mankind have trained themselves for centuries to become fit instruments for discovering the fine workings of the nerves; their records have been published ages ago, colleges have been created to study these subjects, and men and women there are still who are living demonstrations of these phenomena. Of course I admit that there is a good deal of hoax in the whole thing, a good deal of what is wrong and untrue in these things; but with what is this not the case? Take any common scientific phenomenon; there are two or three facts which either scientists or ordinary men may regard as absolute truths, and the rest as mere frothy suppositions. Now let the agnostic apply the same test to his own science which he would apply to what he does not want to believe. Half of it would be shaken to its foundation at once. We are bound to live on suppositions. We cannot live satisfied where we are; that is the natural growth of the human soul. We cannot become agnostics on this side and at the same time go about seeking for anything here; we have to pick. And, for this reason, we have to get beyond our limits, struggle to know what seems to be unknowable; and this struggle must continue.

In my opinion, therefore, I go really one step further than the lecturer, and advance the opinion that most of the psychical phenomena — not only little things like spirit-rappings or table-rappings which are mere child's play, not merely little things like telepathy which I have seen boys do even — most of the psychical phenomenal which the last speaker calls the higher clairvoyance, but which I would rather beg to call the experiences of the superconscious state of the mind, are the very stepping-stones to real psychological investigation. The first thing to be; seen is whether the mind can attain to that state or not. My explanation would, of course, be a little different from his, but we should probably agree when we explain terms. Not much depends on the question whether this present consciousness continues after death or not, seeing that this universe, as it is now, is not bound to this state of consciousness. Consciousness is not co-existent with existence. In my own body, and in all of our bodies, we must all admit that we are conscious of very little of the body, and of the greater part of it we are unconscious. Yet it exists. Nobody is ever conscious of his brain, for example. I never saw my brain, and I am never conscious of it. Yet I know that it exists. Therefore we may say that it is not consciousness that we want, but the existence of something which is not this gross matter; and that that knowledge can be gained even in this life, and that that knowledge has been gained and demonstrated, as far as any science has been demonstrated, is a fact. We have to look into these things, and I would insist on reminding those who are here present on one other point. It is well to remember that very many times we are deluded on this. Certain people place before us the demonstration of a fact which is not ordinary to the spiritual nature, and we reject that fact because we say we cannot find it to be true. In many cases the fact may not be correct. but in many cases also we forget to consider whether we are fit to receive the demonstration or not, whether we have permitted our bodies and our minds to become fit subjects for their discovery.

On Art In India

"Arts and Sciences in India" was the topic under which the Swami Vivekananda was introduced to the audience at Wendte Hall, San Francisco. The Swami held the attention of his hearers throughout as was demonstrated by the many questions which were put to him after his address.

The Swami said in part:

In the history of nations, the government at the beginning has always been in the hands of the priests. All the learning also has proceeded from the priests. Then, after the priests, the government changes hands, and the Kshatriya or the kingly power prevails, and the military rule is triumphant. This has always been true. And last comes the grasp of luxury, and the people sink down under it to be dominated by stronger and more barbarous races.

Amongst all races of the world, from the earliest time in history, India has been called the land of wisdom. For ages India itself has never gone out to conquer other nations. Its people have never been fighters. Unlike your Western people, they do not eat meat, for meat makes fighters; the blood of animals makes you restless, and you desire to do something.

Compare India and England in the Elizabethan period. What a dark age it was for your people, and how enlightened we were even then. The Anglo-Saxon people have always been badly fitted for art. They have good poetry — for instance, how wonderful is the blank verse of Shakespeare! Merely the rhyming of words is not good. It is not the most civilised thing in the world.

In India, music was developed to the full seven notes, even to half and quarter notes, ages ago. India led in music, also in drama and sculpture. Whatever is done now is merely an attempt at imitation. Everything now in India hinges on the question of how little a man requires to live upon.

Is India A Benighted Country?

The following is a report of a lecture at Detroit, United States, America, with the editorial comments of the *Boston Evening Transcript*, 5th April, 1894:

Swami Vivekananda has been in Detroit recently and made a proofed impression there. All classes flocked to hear him, and professional men in particular were greatly interested in his logic and his soundness of thought. The opera-house alone was large enough for his audience. He speaks English extremely well, and he is as handsome as he is good. The Detroit newspapers have devoted much space to the reports of his lectures. An editorial in the *Detroit Evening News* says: Most people will be inclined to think that Swami Vivekananda did better last night in his opera-house lecture than he did in any of his former lectures in this city. The merit of the Hindu's utterances last night lay in their clearness. He drew a very sharp line of distinction between Christianity and Christianity, and told his audience plainly wherein he himself is a Christian in one sense and not a Christian in another sense. He also drew a sharp line between Hinduism and Hinduism, carrying the implication that he desired to be classed as a Hindu only in its better sense. Swami Vivekananda stands superior to all criticism when he says, "We want missionaries of Christ. Let such come to India by the hundreds and thousands. Bring Christ's life to us and let it permeate the very core of society. Let him be preached in every village and corner of India."

When a man is as sound as that on the main question, all else that he may say must refer to the subordinate details. There is infinite humiliation in this spectacle of a pagan priest reading lessons of conduct and of life to the men who have assumed the spiritual supervision of Greenland's icy mountains and India's coral strand; but the sense of humiliation is the *sine qua non* of most reforms in this world. Having said what he did of the glorious life of the author of the Christian faith, Vivekananda has the right to lecture the way he has the men who profess to represent that life among the nations abroad. And after all, how like the Nazarene that sounds: "Provide neither gold nor silver, nor brass in your purses, nor scrip for your journey, neither two coats, neither shoes, nor yet staves; for the workman is worthy of his meat." Those who have become at all familiar with the religious, literature of India before the advent of Vivekananda are best prepared to understand the utter abhorrence of the Orientals of our Western commercial spirit — or what Vivekananda calls, "the shopkeeper's spirit" — in all that we do even in our very religion.

Here is a point for the missionaries which they cannot afford to ignore. They who would convert the Eastern world of paganism must live up to what they preach, in contempt for the kingdoms of this world and all the glory of them.

Brother Vivekananda considers India the most moral nation in the world. Though in bondage, its spirituality still endures. Here are extracts from the notices of some of his recent Detroit addresses: At this point the lecturer struck the great moral keynote of his discourse stating that with his people it was the belief that all non-self is good and all self is bad. This point was emphasised throughout the evening and might be termed the text of the address. "To build a home is selfish, argues the Hindu, so he builds it for the worship of God and for the entertainment of guests. To cook food is selfish, so he cooks it for the poor; he will serve himself last if any hungry stranger applies; and this feeling extends throughout the length and breadth of the land. Any man can ask for food and shelter and any house will be opened to him.

"The caste system has nothing to do with religion. A man's occupation is hereditary — a carpenter is born a carpenter: a goldsmith, a goldsmith; a workman, a workman: and a priest, a priest.

"Two gifts are especially appreciated, the gift of learning and the gift of life. But the gift of learning takes precedence. One may save a man's life, and that is excellent; one may impart to another knowledge, and that is better. To instruct for money is an evil, and to do this would bring opprobrium upon the head of the man who barters learning for gold as though it were an article of trade. The Government makes gifts from time to time to the instructors, and the moral effect is better than it would be if the conditions were the same as exist in certain alleged civilised countries." The speaker had asked throughout the length and breadth of the land what was the definition of "civilization", and he had asked the question in many countries. Sometimes the reply has been, "What we are, that is civilization." He begged to differ in the definition of the word. A nation may conquer the waves, control the elements, develop the utilitarian problems of life seemingly to the utmost limits, and yet not realise that in the individual, the highest type of civilization is found in him who has learned to conquer self. This condition is found more in India than in any other country on earth, for there the material conditions are subservient to the spiritual, and the individual looks to the soul manifestations in everything that has life, studying nature to this end. Hence that gentle disposition to endure with indomitable patience the flings of what appears unkind fortune, the while there is a full consciousness of a spiritual strength and knowledge greater than that possessed by any other people. Therefore the existence of a country and people from which flows an unending stream that attracts the attention of thinkers far and near to approach and throw from their shoulders an oppressive earthly burden.

This lecture was prefaced with the statement that the speaker had been asked many questions. A number of these he preferred to answer privately, but three he had selected for reasons, which would appear, to answer from the pulpit. They were: "Do the people of India throw their children into the jaws of the crocodiles?" "Do they kill themselves beneath the wheels of Jagannâtha?" "Do they burn widows with their husbands?" The first question the lecturer treated in the same vein as an American abroad would in answering inquiries about Indians running round in the streets of New York and similar myths which are even today entertained by many persons on the Continent. The statement was too ludicrous to give a serious response to it. When asked by certain well-meaning but ignorant people why they gave only female children to the crocodiles, he could only ironically reply that probably it was because they were softer and more tender and could be more easily masticated by the inhabitants of the river in that benighted country. Regarding the Jagannatha legend, the lecturer explained the old practice of the Car-festival in the sacred city, and remarked that possibly a few pilgrims in their zeal to grasp the rope and participate in the drawing of the Car slipped and fell and were so destroyed. Some such mishaps had been exaggerated into the distorted versions from which the good people of other countries shrank with horror. Vivekananda denied that people burned widows. It was true, however, that widows had burned themselves. In the few cases where this had happened, they had been urged not to do so by holy men, who were always opposed to suicide. Where the devoted widows insisted, stating that they desired to accompany their husbands in the transformation that had taken place, they were obliged to submit themselves to the fiery tests. That is, they thrust Her hands within the flames, and if they permitted them to be consumed, no further opposition was placed in the way of the fulfilment of their desires. But India is not the only country where women, who have loved, have followed immediately the beloved one to the realms of immortality; suicides in such cases have occurred in every land. It is an uncommon bit of fanaticism in any country — as unusual in India as elsewhere. "No," the speaker repeated, "the people do not burn women in India; nor have they ever burned witches."

This latter touch is decidedly acute by way of reflection. No analysis of the philosophy of the Hindu monk need be attempted here, except to say that it is based in general on the struggle of the soul to individually attain Infinity. One learned Hindu opened the Lowell Institute Course this year. What Mr. Mozoomdar began, might worthily be ended by Brother Vivekananda. This new visitor has by far the most interesting personality, although in the Hindu philosophy, of course, personality is not to be taken into consideration. At the Parliament of Religions they used to keep Vivekananda until the end of the programme to make people stay until the end of the session. On a warm day, when a prosy speaker talked too long and people began going home by hundreds, the Chairman would get up and announce that Swami Vivekananda would make a short address just before the benediction. Then he would have the peaceable hundreds perfectly in tether. The four thousand fanning people in the Hall of Columbus would sit smiling and expectant, waiting for an hour or two of other men's speeches, to listen to Vivekananda for fifteen minutes. The Chairman knew the old rule of keeping the best until the last.

The Claims Of Religion

(Sunday, 5th January)

Many of you remember the thrill of joy with which in your childhood you saw the glorious rising sun; all of you, sometimes in your life, stand and gaze upon the glorious setting sun, and at least in imagination, try to pierce through the beyond. This, in fact, is at the bottom of the whole universe — this rising from and this setting into the beyond, this whole universe coming up out of the unknown, and going back again into the unknown, crawling in as a child out of darkness, and crawling out again as an old man into darkness.

This universe of ours, the universe of the senses, the rational, the intellectual, is bounded on both sides by the illimitable, the unknowable, the ever unknown. Herein is the search, herein art the inquiries, here are the facts; from this comes the light which is known to the world as religion. Essentially, however, religion belongs to the supersensuous and not to the sense plane. It is beyond all reasoning, and not on the plane of intellect. It is a vision, an inspiration, a plunge into the unknown and unknowable making the unknowable more than known, for it can never be "known". This search has been in the human mind, as I believe from the very beginning of humanity. There cannot have been human reasoning and intellect in any period of the world's history without this struggle, this search beyond. In our little universe this human mind, we see a thought arise. Whence it rises we do not know, and when it disappears, where it goes, we know not either. The macrocosm and the microcosm are, as it were in the same groove, passing through the same stages, vibrating in the same key.

I shall try to bring before you the Hindu theory that religions do not come from without, but from within. It is my belief that religious thought is in man's very constitution, so much so that it is impossible for him to give up religion until he can give up his mind and body, until he can stop thought and life. As long as a man thinks, this struggle must go on, and so long man must have some form of religion. Thus we see various forms of religion in the world. It is a bewildering study; but it is not, as many of us think, a vain speculation. Amidst this chaos there is harmony, throughout these discordant sounds there is a note of concord; and he who is prepared to listen to it, will catch the tone.

The great question of all questions at the present time is this: Taking for granted that the knowable and the known are bounded on both sides by the unknowable and the infinitely unknown, why struggle for that unknown? Why shall we not be content with the known? Why shall we not rest satisfied with eating, drinking, and doing a little good to society? This idea is in the air. From the most learned professor to the prattling baby, we are told, "Do good to the world, that is all of religion, and don't bother your head about questions of the beyond." So much so is this the case that it has become a truism.

But fortunately we *must* inquire into the beyond. This present, this expressed, is only one part of that unexpressed. The sense universe is, as it were, only one portion, one bit of that infinite spiritual universe projected into the plane of sense consciousness. How can this little bit of projection be explained, be understood, without knowing that which is beyond? It is said of Socrates that one day while lecturing at Athens, he met a Brâhmana who had travelled into Greece, and Socrates told the Brahmana that the greatest study for mankind is man. And the Brahmana sharply retorted, "How can you know man until you know God?" This God, this eternally Unknowable, or Absolute, or Infinite, or without name — you may call Him by what name you like — is the rationale, the only explanation, the *raison d'etre* of that which is known and knowable, this present life. Take anything before you, the most material thing — take any one of these most materialistic sciences, such as chemistry or physics, astronomy or biology — study it, push the study forward and forward, and the gross forms will begin to melt and become finer and finer, until they come to a point where you are bound to make a tremendous leap from these material things into the immaterial. The gross melts into the fine, physics into metaphysics in every department of knowledge.

So with everything we have — our society, our relations With each other, our religion, and what you call ethics. There are attempts at producing a system of ethics from mere grounds of utility. I challenge any man to produce such a rational system of ethics. Do good to others. Why? Because it is the highest utility. Suppose a man says, "I do not care for utility; I want to cut the throats of others and make myself rich." What will you answer? It is out-Heroding Herod! But where is the utility of my doing good to the world? Am I a fool to work my life out that others may be happy? Why shall I myself not be happy, if there is no other sentiency beyond society, no other power in the universe beyond the five senses? What prevents me from cutting the throats of my brothers so long as I can make myself safe from the police, and make myself happy. What will you answer? You are bound to show some utility. When you are pushed from your ground you answer, "My friend, it is good to be good." What is the power in the human mind which says, "It is good to do good", which unfolds before us in glorious view the grandeur of the soul, the beauty of goodness, the all attractive power of goodness, the infinite power of goodness? That is what we call God. Is it not?

Secondly, I want to tread on a little more delicate ground. I want your attention, and ask you not to make any hasty conclusions from what I say. We cannot do much good to this world. Doing good to the world is very good. But can we do much good to the world? Have we done much good these hundreds of years that we have been struggling — have we increased the sum total of the happiness in the world? Thousands of means have been created every day to conduce to the happiness of the world, and this has been going on for hundreds and thousands of years. I ask you: Is the sum total of the happiness in the world today more than what it divas a century ago? It cannot be. Each wave that rises in the ocean must be at the expense of a hollow somewhere. If one nation becomes rich and powerful, it must be at the expense of another nation somewhere. Each piece of machinery that is invented will make twenty people rich and a twenty thousand people poor. It is the law of competition throughout. The sum total of the energy displayed remains the same throughout. It is, too, a foolhardy task. It is unreasonable to state that we can have happiness without misery. With the increase of all these means, you are increasing the want of the world, and increased wants mean insatiable thirst which will never be quenched. What can fill this want, this thirst? And so long as there is this thirst, misery is inevitable. It is the very nature of life to be happy and miserable by turns. Then again is this world left to you to do good to it? Is there no other power working in this universe? Is God dead and gone, leaving His universe to you and me — the Eternal, the Omnipotent the All-merciful, the Ever-awakened, the One who never sleeps when the universe is sleeping, whose eyes never blink? This infinite sky is, as it were, His ever-open eye. Is He dead and gone? Is He not acting in this universe? It is going on; you need not be in a hurry; you need not make yourself miserable.

[The Swami here told the story of the man who wanted a ghost to work for him, but who, when he had the ghost, could not keep him employed, until he gave him a curly dog's tail to straighten.]

Such is the case with us, with this doing good to the universe. So, my brothers, we are trying to straighten out the tail of the dog these hundreds and thousands of years. It is like rheumatism. You drive it out from the feet, and it goes to the head; you drive it from the head, and it goes somewhere else.

This will seem to many of you to be a terrible, pessimistic view of the world, but it is not. Both pessimism and optimism are wrong. Both are taking up the extremes. So long as a man has plenty to eat and drink, and good clothes to wear, he becomes a great optimist; but that very man, when he loses everything, becomes a great pessimist. When a man loses all his money and is very poor, then and then alone, with the greatest force come to him the ideas of brotherhood of humanity. This is the world, and the more I go to different countries and see of this world, and the older I get, the more I am trying to avoid both these extremes of optimism and pessimism. This world is neither good nor evil. It is the Lord's world. It is beyond both good and evil, perfect in itself. His will is going on, showing all these different pictures; and it will go on without beginning and without end. It is a great gymnasium in which you and I, and millions of souls must come and get exercises, and make ourselves strong and perfect. This is what it is for. Not that God could not make a perfect universe; not that He could not help the misery of the world. You remember the story of the young lady and the clergyman, who were both looking at the moon through the telescope, and found the moon spots. And the clergyman said, "I am sure they are the spires of some churches." "Nonsense," said the young lady, "I am sure they are the young lovers kissing each other." So we are doing with this world. When we are inside, we think we are seeing the inside. According to the plane of existence in which we are, we see the universe. Fire in the kitchen is neither good nor bad. When it cooks a meal for you, you bless the fire, and say, "How good it is!" And when it burns your finger, you say, "What a nuisance it is!" It would be equally correct and logical to say: This universe is neither good nor evil. The world is the world, and will be always so. If we open ourselves to it in such a manner that the action of the world is beneficial to us, we call it good. If we put ourselves in the position in which it is painful, we call it evil. So you will always find children, who are innocent and joyful and do not want to injure anyone, are very optimistic. They are dreaming golden dreams. Old men who have all the desires in their hearts and not the means to fulfil them, and especially those who have been thumped and bumped by the world a good deal, are very pessimistic. Religion wants to know the truth. And the first thing it has discovered is that without a knowledge of this truth there will be no life worth living.

Life will be a desert, human life will be vain, it we cannot know the beyond. It is very good to say: Be contented with tile things of the present moment. The cows and the dogs are, and so are all animals, and that is what makes them animals. So if man rests content with the present and gives up all search into the beyond, mankind will all have to go back to the animal plane again. It is religion, this inquiry into the beyond, that makes the difference between man and an animal. Well has it been said that man is the only animal that naturally looks upwards; every other animal naturally looks down. That looking upward and going upward and seeking perfection are what is called salvation, and the sooner a man begins to go higher, the sooner he raises himself towards this idea of truth as salvation. It does not consist in the amount of money in your pocket, or the dress you wear, or the house You live in, but in the wealth of spiritual thought in your brain. That is what makes for human progress; that is the source of all material and intellectual progress, the motive power behind, the enthusiasm that pushes mankind forward.

What again is the goal of mankind? Is it happiness, sensuous pleasure? They used to say in the olden time that in heaven they will play on trumpets and live round a throne; in modern time I find that they think this ideal is very weak, and they have improved upon it and say that they will have marriages and all these things there. If there is any improvement in these two things, the second is an improvement for the worse. All these various theories of heaven that are being put forward show weakness in the mind. And that weakness is here: First, they think that sense happiness is the goal of life. Secondly, they cannot conceive of anything that is beyond the five senses. They are as irrational as the Utilitarians. Still they are much better than the modern Atheistic Utilitarians, at any rate. Lastly, this Utilitarian position is simply childish. What right have you to say, "Here is my standard, and the whole universe must be governed by my standard?" What right have you to say that every truth shall be judged by this standard of yours — the standard that preaches mere bread, and money, and clothes as God?

Religion does not live in bread, does not dwell in a house. Again and again you hear this objection advanced: "What good can religion do? Can it take away the poverty of the poor and give them more clothes?" Supposing it cannot, would that prove the untruth of religion? Suppose a baby stands up among you, when you are trying to demonstrate an astronomical theory, and says, "Does it bring gingerbread?" "No, it does not," you answer. "Then," says the baby, "it is useless." Babies judge the whole universe from their own standpoint, that of producing gingerbread, and so do the babies of the world.

Sad to say at the later end of this nineteenth century that these are passing for the learned, the most rational, the most logical, the most intelligent crowd ever seen on this earth.

We must not judge of higher things from this low standpoint of ours. Everything must be judged by its own standard, and the infinite must be judged by the standard of infinity. Religion permeates the whole of man's life, not only the present, but the past, present, and future. It is therefore the eternal relation between the eternal Soul, and the eternal God. Is it logical to measure its value by its action upon five minutes of human life? Certainly not. But these are all negative arguments.

Now comes the question: Can religion really do anything? It can.

Can religion really bring bread and clothes? It does. It is always doing so, and it does infinitely more than that; it brings to man eternal life. It has made man what he is, and will make of this human animal a God. That is what religion can do. Take off religion from human society, what will remain? Nothing but a forest of brutes. As I have just tried to show you that it is absurd to suppose that sense happiness is the goal of humanity, we find as a conclusion that knowledge is the goal of all life. I have tried to show to you that in these thousands of years of struggle for the search of truth and the benefit of mankind, we have scarcely made the least appreciable advance. But mankind has made gigantic advance in knowledge. The highest utility of this progress lies not in the creature comforts that it brings, but in manufacturing a god out of this animal man. Then, with knowledge, naturally comes bliss. Babies think that the happiness of the senses is the highest thing they can have. Most of you know that there is a keener enjoyment in man in the intellect, than in the senses. No one of you can feel the same pleasure in eating as a dog does. You can mark that. Where does the pleasure come from in man? Not that whole-souled enjoyment of eating that the pig or the dog has. See how the pig eats. It is unconscious of the universe while it is eating; its whole soul is bound up in the food. It may be killed but it does not care when it has food. Think of the intense enjoyment that the pig has! No man has that. Where is it gone? Man has changed it into intellectual enjoyment. The pig cannot enjoy religious lectures. That is one step higher and keener yet than intellectual pleasures, and that is the spiritual plane, spiritual enjoyment of things divine, soaring beyond reason and intellect. To procure that we shall have to lose all these sense-enjoyments. This is the highest utility. Utility is what I enjoy, and what everyone enjoys, and we run for that.

We find that man enjoys his intellect much more than an animal enjoys his senses, and we see that man enjoys his spiritual nature even more than his rational nature. So the highest wisdom must be this spiritual knowledge. With this knowledge will come bliss. All these things of this world are but the shadows, the manifestations in the third or fourth degree of the real Knowledge and Bliss.

It is this Bliss that comes to you through the love of humanity; the shadow of this spiritual Bliss is this human love, but do not confound it with that human bliss. There is that great error: We are always mistaking the: love that we have — this carnal, human love, this attachment for particles, this electrical attraction for human beings in society — for this spiritual Bliss. We are apt to mistake this for that eternal state, which it is not. For want of any other name in English, I would call it Bliss, which is the same as eternal knowledge — and that is our goal. Throughout the world, wherever there has been a religion, and wherever there will be a religion, they have all sprung and will all spring out of one source, called by various names in various countries; and that is what in the Western countries you call "inspiration". What is this inspiration? Inspiration is the only source of religious knowledge. We have seen that religion essentially belongs to the plane beyond the senses. It is "where the eyes cannot go, or the ears, where the mind cannot reach, or what words cannot express". That is the field and goal of religion, and from this comes that which we call inspiration. It naturally follows, therefore, that there must be some way to go beyond the senses. It is perfectly true that our reason cannot go beyond the senses; all reasoning is within the senses, and reason is based upon the facts which the senses reach. But can a man go beyond the senses? Can a man know the unknowable? Upon this the whole question of religion is to be and has been decided. From time immemorial there was that adamantine wall, the barrier to the senses; from time immemorial hundreds and thousands of men and women haven't dashed themselves against this wall to penetrate beyond. Millions have failed, and millions have succeeded. This is the history of the world. Millions more do not believe that anyone ever succeeded; and these are the sceptics of the present day. Man succeeds in going beyond this wall if he only tries. Man has not only reason, he has not only senses, but there is much in him which is beyond the senses. We shall try to explain it a little. I hope you will feel that it is within you also.

I move my hand, and I feel and I know that I am moving my hand. I call it consciousness. I am conscious that I am moving my hand. But my heart is moving. I am not conscious of that; and yet who is moving the heart? It must be the same being. So we see that this being who moves the hands and speaks, that is to say, acts consciously, also acts unconsciously. We find, therefore, that this being can act upon two planes — one, the plane of consciousness, and the other, the plane below that. The impulsions from the plane of unconsciousness are what we call instinct, and when the same impulsions come from the plane of consciousness, we call it reason. But there is a still higher plane, superconsciousness in man. This is apparently the same as unconsciousness, because it is beyond the plane of consciousness, but it is above consciousness and not below it. It is not instinct, it is inspiration. There is proof of it. Think of all these great prophets and sages that the world has produced, and it is well known how there will be times in their lives, moments in their existence, when they will be apparently unconscious of the external world; and all the knowledge that subsequently comes out of them, they claim, was gained during this state of existence. It is said of Socrates that while marching with the army, there was a beautiful sunrise, and that set in motion in his mind a train of thought; he stood there for two days in the sun quite unconscious. It was such moments that gave the Socratic knowledge to the world. So with all the great preachers and prophets, there are moments in their lives when they, as it were, rise from the conscious and go above it. And when they come back to the plane of consciousness, they come radiant with light; they have brought news from the beyond, and they are the inspired seers of the world.

But there is a great danger. Any man may say he is inspired; many times they say that. Where is the test? During sleep we are unconscious; a fool goes to sleep; he sleeps soundly for three hours; and when he comes back from that state, he is the same fool if not worse. Jesus of Nazareth goes into his transfiguration, and when he comes out, he has become Jesus the Christ. That is all the difference. One is inspiration, and the other is instinct. The one is a child, and the other is the old experienced man. This inspiration is possible for everyone of us. It is the source of all religions, and will ever be the source of all higher knowledge. Yet there are great dangers in the way. Sometimes fraudulent people try to impose themselves upon mankind. In these days it is becoming all too prevalent. A friend of mine had a very fine picture. Another gentleman who was rather religiously inclined, and a rich man, had his eyes upon this picture; but my friend would not sell it. This other gentleman one day comes and says to my friend, I have an inspiration and I have a message from God. "What is your message?" my friend asked. "The message is that you must deliver that picture to me." My friend was up to his mark; he immediately added, "Exactly so; how beautiful! I had exactly the same inspiration, that I should have to deliver to you the picture. Have you brought your cheque?" "Cheque? What cheque?' "Then", said my friend, "I don't think your inspiration was right. My inspiration was that I must give the picture to the man who brought a cheque for $100,000. You must bring the cheque first." The other man found he was caught, and gave up the inspiration theory. These are the dangers. A man came to me in Boston and said he had visions in which he had been talked to in the Hindu language. I said, "If I can see what he says I will believe it." But he wrote down a lot of nonsense. I tried my best to understand it, but I could not. I told him that so far as my knowledge went, such language never was and never will be in India. They had not become civilised enough to have such a language as that. He thought of course that I was a rogue and sceptic, and went away; and I would not be surprised next to hear that he was in a lunatic asylum. These are the two dangers always in this world — the danger from frauds, and the danger from fools. But that need not deter us, for all great things in this world are fraught with danger. At the same time we must take a little precaution. Sometimes I find persons perfectly wanting in logical analysis of anything. A man comes and says, "I have a message from such and such a god", and asks, "Can you deny it? Is it not possible that there will be such and such a god, and that he will give such a message? And 90 per cent of fools will swallow it. They think that that is reason enough. But one thing you ought to know, that it is possible for anything to happen - quite possible that the earth may come into contact with the Dog star in the next year and go to pieces. But if I advance this proposition, you have the right to stand up and ask me to prove it to you. What the lawyers call the *onus probandi* is on the man who made the proposition. It is not your duty to prove that I got my inspiration from a certain god, but mine, because I produced the proposition to you. If I cannot prove it, I should better hold my tongue. Avoid both these dangers, and you can get anywhere you please. Many of us get many messages in our lives, or think we get them, and as long as the message is regarding our own selves, go on doing what you please; but when it is in regard to our contact with and behaviour to others, think a hundred times before you act upon it; and then you will be safe.

We find that this inspiration is the only source of religion; yet it has always been fraught with many dangers; and the last and worst of all dangers is excessive claims. Certain men stand up and say they have a communication from God, and they are the mouthpiece of God Almighty, and no one else has the right to have that communication. This, on the face of it, is unreasonable. If there is anything in the universe, it must be universal; there is not one movement here that is not universal, because the whole universe is governed by laws. It is systematic and harmonious all through. Therefore what is anywhere must be everywhere. Each atom in the universe is built on the same plan as the biggest sun and the stars. If one man was ever inspired, it is possible for each and every one of us to be inspired, and that is religion. Avoid all these dangers, illusions and delusions, and fraud and making excessive claims, but come face to face with religious facts, and come into direct contact with the science of religion. Religion does not consist in believing any number of doctrines or dogmas, in going to churches or temples, in reading certain books. Have you seen God? Have you seen the soul? If not, are you struggling for it? It is here and now, and you have not to wait for the future. What is the future but the present illimitable? What is the whole amount of time but one second repeated again and again? Religion is here and now, in this present life.

One question more: What is the goal? Nowadays it is asserted that man is progressing infinitely, forward and forward, and there is no goal of perfection to attain to. Ever approaching, never attaining, whatever that may mean, and however wonderful it may be, it is absurd on the face of it. Is there any motion in a straight line? A straight line infinitely projected becomes a circle, it returns back to the starting point. You must end where you begin; and as you began in God, you must go back to God. What remains? Detail work. Through eternity you have to do the detail work.

Yet another question: Are we to discover new truths of religion as we go on? Yea and nay. In the first place, we cannot know anything more of religion; it has been all known. In all the religions of the world you will find it claimed that there is a unity within us. Being one with the Divinity, there cannot be any further progress in that sense. Knowledge means finding this unity in variety. I see you as men and women, and this is variety. It becomes scientific knowledge when I group you together and call you human beings. Take the science of chemistry, for instance. Chemists are seeking to resolve all known substances into their original elements, and if possible, to find the one element from which all these are derived. The time may come when they will find the one element. That is the source of all other elements. Reaching that, they can go no further; the science of chemistry will have become perfect. So it is with the science of religion. If we can discover this perfect unity, then there cannot be any further progress.

When it was discovered that "I and my Father are one", the last word was said of religion. Then there only remained detail work. In true religion there is no faith or belief in the sense of blind faith. No great preacher ever preached that. That only comes with degeneracy. Fools pretend to be followers of this or that spiritual giant, and although they may be without power, endeavour to teach humanity to believe blindly. Believe what? To believe blindly is to degenerate the human soul. Be an atheist if you want, but do not believe in anything unquestioningly. Why degrade the soul to the level of animals? You not only hurt yourselves thereby, but you injure society, and make danger for those that come after you. Stand up and reason out, having no blind faith. Religion is a question of being and becoming, not of believing. This is religion, and when you have attained to that you have religion. Before that you are no better than the animals. "Do not believe in what you have heard," says the great Buddha, "do not believe in doctrines because they have been handed down to you through generations; do not believe in anything because it is followed blindly by many; do not believe because some old sage makes a statement; do not believe in truths to which you have become attached by habit; do not believe merely on the authority of your teachers and elders. Have deliberation and analyse, and when the result agrees with reason and conduces to the good of one and all, accept it and live up to it."

Concentration

(Delivered at the Washington Hall, San Francisco, on March 16, 1900)

[This and the following two lectures (Meditation and The Practice of Religion) are reproduced here from the *Vedanta and the West* with the kind permission of the Vedanta Society of Southern California, by whom is reserved the copyright for America. The lectures were recorded by Ida Ansell under circumstances which she herself relates thus:

"Swami Vivekananda's second trip to the West occurred in 1899-1900. During the first half of 1900 he worked in and around San Francisco, California. I was a resident of that city, twenty-two years old at the time. ... I heard him lecture perhaps a score of times from March to May of 1900, and recorded seventeen of his talks. ...

"The lectures were given in San Francisco, Oakland, and Alameda, in churches, in the Alameda and San Francisco Homes of Truth, and in rented halls. ... Altogether Swamiji gave, besides nearly daily interviews and informal classes, at least thirty or forty major addresses in March, April, and May. ...

"I was long hesitant about transcribing and releasing these lectures because of the imperfectness of my notes. I was just an amateur stenographer, at the time I took them. ... One would have needed a speed of at least three hundred words per minute to capture all of Swamiji's torrents of eloquence. I possessed less than half the required speed, and at the time I had no idea that the material would have value to anyone but myself. In addition to his fast speaking pace, Swamiji was a superb actor. His stories and imitations absolutely forced one to stop writing, to enjoy watching him. ... Even though my notes were somewhat fragmentary, I have yielded to the opinion that their contents are precious and must be given for publication.

Swamiji's speaking style was colloquial, fresh, and forceful. No alterations have been made in it; no adjusting or smoothing out of his spontaneous flow for purposes of publication has been done. Where omissions were made because of some obscurity in the meaning, they have been indicated by three dots. Anything inserted for purposes of clarification has been placed in square brackets. With these qualifications, the words are exactly as Swamiji spoke them.

Everything Swamiji said had tremendous power. These lectures have slept in my old stenographer's notebook for more than fifty years. Now as they emerge, one feels that the power is still there."]

All knowledge that we have, either of the external or internal world, is obtained through only one method — by the concentration of the mind. No knowledge can be had of any science unless we can concentrate our minds upon the subject. The astronomer concentrates his mind through the telescope... and so on. If you want to study your own mind, it will be the same process. You will have to concentrate your mind and turn it back upon itself. The difference in this world between mind and mind is simply the fact of concentration. One, more concentrated than the other, gets more knowledge.

In the lives of all great men, past and present, we find this tremendous power of concentration. Those are men of genius, you say. The science of Yoga tells us that we are all geniuses if we try hard to be. Some will come into this life better fitted and will do it quicker perhaps. We can all do the same. The same power is in everyone. The subject of the present lecture is how to concentrate the mind in order to study the mind itself. Yogis have laid down certain rules and this night I am going to give you a sketch of some of these rules.

Concentration, of course, comes from various sources. Through the senses you can get concentration. Some get it when they hear beautiful music, others when they see beautiful scenery. ... Some get concentrated by lying upon beds of spikes, sharp iron spikes, others by sitting upon sharp pebbles. These are extraordinary cases [using] most unscientific procedure. Scientific procedure is gradually training the mind.

One gets concentrated by holding his arm up. Torture gives him the concentration he wants. But all these are extraordinary.

Universal methods have been organised according to different philosophers. Some say the state we want to attain is superconsciousness of the mind — going beyond the limitations the body has made for us. The value of ethics to the Yogi lies in that it makes the mind pure. The purer the mind, the easier it is to control it. The mind takes every thought that rises and works it out. The grosser the mind, the more difficult [it is] to control

[it]. The immoral man will never be able to concentrate his mind to study psychology. He may get a little control as he begins, get a little power of hearing. ... and even those powers will go from him. The difficulty is that if you study closely, you see how [the] extraordinary power arrived at was not attained by regular scientific training. The men who, by the power of magic, control serpents will be killed by serpents. ... The man who attains any extraordinary powers will in the long run succumb to those powers. There are millions [who] receive power through all sorts of ways in India. The vast majority of them die raving lunatics. Quite a number commit suicide, the mind [being] unbalanced.

The study must be put on the safe side: scientific, slow, peaceful. The first requisite is to be moral. Such a man wants the gods to come down, and they will come down and manifest themselves to him. That is our psychology and philosophy in essence, [to be] perfectly moral. Just think what that means! No injury, perfect purity, perfect austerity! These are absolutely necessary. Just think, if a man can attain all these in perfection! What more do you want? If he is free from all enmity towards any being, ... all animals will give up their enmity [in his presence]. The Yogis lay down very strict laws... so that one cannot pass off for a charitable man without; being charitable. ...

If you believe me, I have seen a man [The reference is evidently to Pavhari Baba (see Sketch of the Life of Pavhari Baba in this volume)] who used to live in a hole and there were cobras and frogs living with him. ... Sometimes he would fast for [days and months] and then come out. He was always silent. One day there came a robber. ...

My old master used to say, "When the lotus of the heart has bloomed, the bees will come by themselves." Men like that are there yet. They need not talk. ... When the man is perfect from his heart, without a thought of hatred, all animals will give up their hatred [before him]. So with purity. These are necessary for our dealings with our fellow beings. We must love all. ... We have no business to look at the faults of others: it does no good We must not even think of them. Our business is with the good. We are not here to deal with faults. Our business is to be good.

Here comes Miss So-and-so. She says, "I am going to be a Yogi." She tells the news twenty times, meditates fifty days, then she says, "There is nothing in this religion. I have tried it. There is nothing in it."

The very basis [of spiritual life] is not there. The foundation [must be] this perfect morality. That is the great difficulty. ...

In our country there are vegetarian sects. They will take in the early morning pounds of sugar and place it on the ground for ants, and the story is, when one of them was putting sugar on the ground for ants, a man placed his foot upon the ants. The former said, "Wretch, you have killed the animals!" And he gave him such a blow, that it killed the man.

External purity is very easy and all the world rushes towards [it]. If a certain kind of dress is the kind of morality [to be observed], any fool can do that. When it is grappling with the mind itself, it is hard work.

The people who do external, superficial things are so self-righteous! I remember, when I was a boy I had great regard for the character of Jesus Christ. [Then I read about the wedding feast in the Bible.] I closed the book and said, "He ate meat and drank wine! He cannot be a good man."

We are always losing sight of the real meaning of things. The little eating and dress! Every fool can see that. Who sees that which is beyond? It is culture of the heart that we want. ... One mass of people in India we see bathing twenty times a day sometimes, making themselves very pure. And they do not touch anyone. ... The coarse facts, the external things! [If by bathing one could be pure,] fish are the purest beings.

Bathing, and dress, and food regulation — all these have their proper value when they are complementary to the spiritual. .... That first, and these all help. But without it, no amount of eating grass... is any good at all. They are helps if properly understood. But improperly understood, they are derogatory. ...

This is the reason why I am explaining these things: First, because in all religions everything degenerates upon being practiced by [the ignorant]. The camphor in the bottle evaporated, and they are fighting over the bottle.

Another thing: ... [Spirituality] evaporates when they say, "This is right, and that is wrong." All quarrels are [with forms and creeds] never in the spirit. The Buddhist offered for years glorious preaching; gradually, this spirituality evaporated. ... [Similarly with Christianity.] And then began the quarrel whether it is three gods in one or one in three, when nobody wants to go to God Himself and know what He is. We have to go to God Himself to know whether He is three in one or one in three.

Now, with this explanation, the posture. Trying to control the mind, a certain posture is necessary. Any posture in which the person can sit easily — that is the posture for that person. As a rule, you will find that the spinal column must be left free. It is not intended to bear the weight of the body.

... The only thing to remember in the sitting posture: [use] any posture in which the spine is perfectly free of the weight of the body.

Next [Prânâyâma] ... the breathing exercises. A great deal of stress is laid upon breathing. ... What I am telling you is not something gleaned from some sect in India. It is universally true. Just as in this country you teach your children certain prayers, [in India] they get the children and give them certain facts etc.

Children are not taught any religion in India except one or two prayers. Then they begin to seek for somebody with whom they can get *en rapport*. They go to different persons and find that "This man is the man for me", and get initiation. If I am married, my wife may possibly get another man teacher and my son will get somebody else, and that is always my secret between me and my teacher. The wife's religion the husband need not know, and he would not dare ask her what her religion is. It is well known that they would never say. It is only known to that person and the teacher. ... Sometimes you will find that what would be quite ludicrous to one will be just teaching for another. ... Each is carrying his own burden and is to be helped according to his particular mind. It is the business of every individual, between him, his teacher, and God. But there are certain general methods which all these teachers preach. Breathing [and] meditating are universal. That is the worship in India.

On the banks of the Gangâ, we will see men, women, and children all [practicing] breathing and then meditating. Of course, they have other things to do. They cannot devote much time to this. But those who have taken this as the study of life, they practice various methods. There are eighty-four different Âsanas (postures). Those that take it up under some person, they always feel the breath and the movements in all the different parts of the body. ...

Next comes Dhâranâ [concentration]. ... Dharana is holding the mind in certain spots.

The Hindu boy or girl ... gets initiation. He gets from his Guru a word. This is called the root word. This word is given to the Guru [by his Guru], and he gives it to his disciple. One such word is OM. All these symbols have a great deal of meaning, and they hold it secret, never write it. They must receive it through the ear – not through writing – from the teacher, and then hold it as God himself. Then they meditate on the word. ...

I used to pray like that at one time, all through the rainy season, four months. I used to get up and take a plunge in the river, and with all my wet clothes on repeat [the Mantra] till the sun set. Then I ate something — a little rice or something. Four months in the rainy season!

The Indian mind believes that there is nothing in the world that cannot be obtained. If a man wants money in this country, he goes to work and earns money. There, he gets a formula and sits under a tree and believes that money must come. Everything must come by the power of his [thought]. You make money here. It is the same thing. You put forth your whole energy upon money making.

There are some sects called Hatha-Yogis. ... They say the greatest good is to keep the body from dying. ... Their whole process is clinging to the body. Twelve years training! And they begin with little children, others wise it is impossible. ... One thing [is] very curious about the Hatha-Yogi: When he first becomes a disciple, he goes into the wilderness and lives alone forty days exactly. All they have they learn within those forty days. ...

A man in Calcutta claims to have lived five hundred years. The people all tell me that their grandfathers saw him. ... He takes a constitutional twenty miles, never walks, he runs. Goes into the water, covers himself [from] top to toe with mud. After that he plunges again into the water, again sticks himself with mud. ... I do not see any good in that. (Snakes, they say, live two hundred years.) He must be very old, because I have travelled fourteen years in India and wherever I went everybody knew him. He has been travelling all his life. ... [The Hatha-Yogi] will swallow a piece of rubber eighty inches long and take it out again. Four times a day he has to wash every part of his body, internal and external parts. ...

The walls can keep their bodies thousands of years. ... What of that? I would not want to live so long. "Sufficient unto the day is the evil thereof." One little body, with all its delusions and limitations, is enough.

There are other sects. ... They give you a drop of the elixir of life and you remain young. ... It will take me months to enumerate [all the sects]. All their activity is on this side [in the material world]. Every day a new sect. ...

The power of all those sects is in the mind. Their idea is to hold the mind. First concentrate it and hold it at a certain place. They generally say, at certain parts of the body along the spinal column or upon the nerve centres. By holding the mind at the nerve centres, [the Yogi] gets power over the body. The body is the great cause of disturbance to his peace, is opposite of his highest ideal, so he wants control: [to] keep the body as servant.

Then comes meditation. That is the highest state. ... When [the mind] is doubtful that is not its great state. Its great state is meditation. It looks upon things and sees things, not identifying itself with anything else. As long as I feel pain, I have identified myself with the body. When I feel joy or pleasure, I have identified myself with the body. But the high state will look with the same pleasure or blissfulness upon pleasure or upon pain. ... Every meditation is direct superconsciousness. In perfect concentration the soul becomes actually free from the bonds of the gross body and knows itself as it is. Whatever one wants, that comes to him. Power and knowledge are already there. The soul identifies itself with that which is powerless matter and thus weeps. It identifies itself with mortal shapes. ... But if that free soul wants to exercise any power, it will have it. If it does not, it does not come. He who has known God has become God. There is nothing impossible to such a free soul. No more birth and death for him. He is free for ever.

Meditation

(Delivered at the Washington Hall, San Francisco, April 3, 1900)*

Meditation has been laid stress upon by all religions. The meditative state of mind is declared by the Yogis to be the highest state in which the mind exists. When the mind is studying the external object, it gets identified with it, loses itself. To use the simile of the old Indian philosopher: the soul of man is like a piece of crystal, but it takes the colour of whatever is near it. Whatever the soul touches ... it has to take its colour. That is the difficulty. That constitutes the bondage. The colour is so strong, the crystal forgets itself and identifies itself with the colour. Suppose a red flower is near the crystal and the crystal takes the colour and forgets itself, thinks it is red. We have taken the colour of the body and have forgotten what we are. All the difficulties that follow come from that one dead body. All our fears, all worries, anxieties, troubles, mistakes, weakness, evil, are front that one great blunder — that we are bodies. This is the ordinary person. It is the person taking the colour of the flower near to it. We are no more bodies than the crystal is the red flower.

The practice of meditation is pursued. The crystal knows what it is, takes its own colour. It is meditation that brings us nearer to truth than anything else. ...

In India two persons meet. In English they say, "How do you do?" The Indian greeting is, "Are you upon yourself?" The moment you stand upon something else, you run the risk of being miserable. This is what I mean by meditation — the soul trying to stand upon itself. That state must surely be the healthiest state of the soul, when it is thinking of itself, residing in its own glory. No, all the other methods that we have — by exciting emotions, prayers, and all that — really have that one end in view. In deep emotional excitement the soul tries to stand upon itself. Although the emotion may arise from anything external, there is concentration of mind.

There are three stages in meditation. The first is what is called [Dhâranâ], concentrating the mind upon an object. I try to concentrate my mind upon this glass, excluding every other object from my mind except this glass. But the mind is wavering . . . When it has become strong and does not waver so much, it is called [Dhyâna], meditation. And then there is a still higher state when the differentiation between the glass and myself is lost — [Samâdhi or absorption]. The mind and the glass are identical. I do not see any difference. All the senses stop and all powers that have been working through other channels of other senses [are focused in the mind]. Then this glass is under the power of the mind entirely. This is to be realised. It is a tremendous play played by the Yogis. ... Take for granted, the external object exists. Then that which is really outside of us is not what we see. The glass that I see is not the external object certainly. That external something which is the glass I do not know and will never know.

Something produces an impression upon me. Immediately I send the reaction towards that, and the glass is the result of the combination of these two. Action from outside — X. Action from inside — Y. The glass is XY. When you look at X, call it external world — at Y, internal world . . . If you try to distinguish which is your mind and which is the world — there is no such distinction. The world is the combination of you and something else. ...

Let us take another example. You are dropping stones upon the smooth surface of a lake. Every stone you drop is followed by a reaction. The stone is covered by the little waves in the lake. Similarly, external things are like the stones dropping into the lake of the mind. So we do not really see the external . . .; we see the wave only. . . .

These waves that rise in the mind have caused many things outside. We are not discussing the [merits of] idealism and realism. We take for granted that things exist outside, but what we see is different from things that exist outside, as we see what exists outside plus ourselves.

Suppose I take my contribution out of the glass. What remains? Almost nothing. The glass will disappear. If I take my contribution from the table, what would remain of the table? Certainly not this table, because it was a mixture of the outside plus my contribution. The poor lake has got to throw the wave towards the stone whenever [the stone] is thrown in it. The mind must create the wave towards any sensation. Suppose . . . we can withhold the mind. At once we are masters. We refuse to contribute our share to all these phenomena.... If I do not contribute my share, it has got to stop.

You are creating this bondage all the time. How? By putting in your share. We are all making our own beds, forging our own chains.... When the identifying ceases between this external object and myself, then I will be able to take my contribution off, and this thing will disappear. Then I will say, "Here is the glass", and then take my mind off, and it disappears....

If you can take away your share, you can walk upon water. Why should it drown you any more? What of poison? No more difficulties. In every phenomenon in nature you contribute at least half, and nature brings half. If your half is taken off, the thing must stop.

... To every action there is equal reaction.... If a man strikes me and wounds me it is that man's actions and my body's reaction. ... Suppose I have so much power over the body that I can resist even that automatic action. Can such power be attained? The books say it can. ... If you stumble on [it], it is a miracle. If you learn it scientifically, it is Yoga.

I have seen people healed by the power of mind. There is the miracle worker. We say he prays and the man is healed. Another man says, "Not at all. It is just the power of the mind. The man is scientific. He knows what he is about."

The power of meditation gets us everything. If you want to get power over nature, [you can have it through meditation]. It is through the power of meditation all scientific facts are discovered today. They study the subject and forget everything, their own identity and everything, and then the great fact comes like a flash. Some people think that is inspiration. There is no more inspiration than there is expiration; and never was anything got for nothing.

The highest so-called inspiration was the work of Jesus. He worked hard for ages in previous births. That was the result of his previous work — hard work. ... It is all nonsense to talk about inspiration. Had it been, it would have fallen like rain. Inspired people in any line of thought only come among nations who have general education and [culture]. There is no inspiration. . . . Whatever passes for inspiration is the result that comes from causes already in the mind. One day, flash comes the result! Their past work was the [cause].

Therein also you see the power of meditation — intensity of thought. These men churn up their own souls. Great truths come to the surface and become manifest. Therefore the practice of meditation is the great scientific method of knowledge. There is no knowledge without the power of meditation. From ignorance, superstition, etc. we can get cured by meditation for the time being and no more. [Suppose] a man has told me that if you drink such a poison you will be killed, and another man comes in the night and says, "Go drink the poison!" and I am not killed, [what happens is this:] my mind cut out from the meditation the identity between the poison and myself just for the time being. In another case of [drinking] the poison, I will be killed.

If I know the reason and scientifically raise myself up to that [state of meditation], I can save anyone. That is what the books say; but how far it is correct you must appraise.

I am asked, "Why do you Indian people not conquer these things? You claim all the time to be superior to all other people. You practice Yoga and do it quicker than anybody else. You are fitter. Carry it out! If you are a great people, you ought to have a great system. You will have to say good-bye to all the gods. Let them go to sleep as you take up the great philosophers. You are mere babies, as superstitious as the rest of the world. And all your claims are failures. If you have the claims, stand up and be bold, and all the heaven that ever existed is yours. There is the musk deer with fragrance inside, and he does not know where the fragrance [comes from]. Then after days and days he finds it in himself. All these gods and demons are within them. Find out, by the powers of reason, education, and culture that it is all in yourself. No more gods and superstitions. You want to be rational, to be Yogis, really spiritual."

[My reply is: With you too] everything is material What is more material than God sitting on a throne? You look down upon the poor man who is worshipping the image. You are no better. And you, gold worshippers, what are you? The image worshipper worships his god, something that he can see. But you do not even do that. You do not worship the spirit nor something that you can understand. ... Word worshippers! "God is spirit!" God *is* spirit and should be worshipped in spirit and faith. Where does the spirit reside? On a tree? On a cloud? What do you mean by God being *ours*? *You are* the spirit. That is the first fundamental belief you must never give up. I am the spiritual being. It is there. All this skill of Yoga and this system of meditation and everything is just to find Him there.

Why am I saying all this just now? Until you fix the location, you cannot talk. You fix it up in heaven and all the world ever except in the right place. I am spirit, and therefore the spirit of all spirits must be in my soul. Those who think it anywhere else are ignorant. Therefore it is to be sought here in this heaven; all the heaven that ever existed [is within myself]. There are some sages who, knowing this, turn their eyes inward and find the spirit of all spirits in their own spirit. That is the scope of meditation. Find out the truth about God and about your own soul and thus attain to liberation. ...

You are all running after life, and we find that is foolishness. There is something much higher than life even. This life is inferior, material. Why should I live at all? I am something higher than life. Living is always slavery. We always get mixed up. ... Everything is a continuous chain of slavery.

You get something, and no man can teach another. It is through experience [we learn]. ... That young man cannot be persuaded that there are any difficulties in life. You cannot persuade the *old* man that life is all smooth. He has had many experiences. That is the difference.

By the power of meditation we have got to control, step by step, all these things. We have seen philosophically that all these differentiations — spirit, mind, matter, etc. — [have no real existences. ... Whatever exists is one. There cannot be many. That is what is meant by science and knowledge. Ignorance sees manifold. Knowledge realises one. ... Reducing the many into one is science. ... The whole of the universe has been demonstrated into one. That science is called the science of Vedanta. The whole universe is one. The one runs through all this seeming variety. ...

We have all these variations now and we see them — what we call the five elements: solid, liquid, gaseous, luminous, ethereal. After that the state of existence is mental and beyond that spiritual. Not that spirit is one and mind is another, ether another, and so on. It is the one existence appearing in all these variations. To go back, the solid must become liquid. The way [the elements evolved] they must go back. The solids will become liquid, etherised. This is the idea of the macrocosm — and universal. There is the external universe and universal spirit, mind, ether, gas, luminosity, liquid, solid.

The same with the mind. I am just exactly the same in the microcosm. I am the spirit; I am mind; I am the ether, solid, liquid, gas. What I want to do is to go back to my spiritual state. It is for the individual to live the life of the universe in one short life. Thus man can be free in this life. He in his own short lifetime shall have the power to live the whole extent of life....

We all struggle. . . . . If we cannot reach the Absolute, we will get somewhere, and it will be better than we are now.

Meditation consists in this practice [of dissolving every thing into the ultimate Reality — spirit]. The solid melts into liquid, that into gas, gas into ether, then mind, and mind will melt away. All is spirit.

Some of the Yogis claim that this body will become liquid etc. You will be able to do any thing with it — make it little, or gas pass through this wall — they claim. I do not know. I have never seen anybody do it. But it is in the books. We have no reason to disbelieve the books.

Possibly, some of us will be able to do it in this life. Like a flash it comes, as the result of our past work. Who knows but some here are old Yogis with just a little to do to finish the whole work. Practice!

Meditation, you know, comes by a process imagination. You go through all these processes purification of the elements — making the one melt the other, that into the next higher, that into mind, that into spirit, and then you are spirit.

Spirit is always free, omnipotent, omniscient. Of course, under God. There cannot be many Gods. These liberated souls are wonderfully powerful, almost omnipotent. [But] none can be as powerful as God. If one [liberated soul] said, "I will make this planet go this way", and another said, "I will make it go that way", [there would be confusion].

Don't you make this mistake! When I say in English, "I am God!" it is because I have no better word. In Sanskrit, God means absolute existence, knowledge, and wisdom, infinite self-luminous consciousness. No person. It is impersonal. ...

I am never Râma [never one with Ishvara, the personal aspect of God], but I am [one with Brahman, the impersonal, all-pervading existence]. Here is a huge mass of clay. Out of that clay I made a little [mouse] and you made a little [elephant]. Both are clay. Melt both down They are essentially one. "I and my Father are one." [But the clay mouse can never be one with the clay elephant.]

I stop somewhere; I have a little knowledge. You a little more; you stop somewhere. There is one soul which is the greatest of all. This is Ishvara, Lord of Yoga [God as Creator, with attributes]. He is the individual. He is omnipotent. He resides in every heart. There is no body. He does not need a body. All you get by the practice of meditation etc., you can get by meditation upon Ishvara, Lord of Yogis. ...

The same can be attained by meditating upon a great soul; or upon the harmony of life. These are called objective meditations. So you begin to meditate upon certain external things, objective things, either outside or inside. If you take a long sentence, that is no meditation at all. That is simply trying to get the mind collected by repetition. Meditation means the mind is turned back upon itself. The mind stops all the [thought-waves] and the world stops. Your consciousness expands. Every time you meditate you will keep your growth. ... Work a little harder, more and more, and meditation comes. You do not feel the body or anything else. When you come out of it after the hour, you have had the most beautiful rest you ever had in your life. That is the only way you ever give rest to your system. Not even the deepest sleep will give you such rest as that. The mind goes on jumping even in deepest sleep. Just those few minutes [in meditation] your brain has almost stopped. Just a little vitality is kept up. You forget the body. You may be cut to pieces and not feel it at all. You feel such pleasure in it. You become so light. This perfect rest we will get in meditation.

Then, meditation upon different objects. There are meditations upon different centres of the spine. [According to the Yogis, there are two nerves in the spinal column, called Idâ and Pingalâ.They are the main channels through which the afferent and efferent currents travel.] The hollow [canal called Sushumnâ] runs through the middle of the spinal column. The Yogis claim this cord is closed, but by the power of meditation it has to be opened. The energy has to be sent down to [the base of the spine], and the Kundalini rises. The world will be changed. ... (See Complete Works, Vol. I)

Thousands of divine beings are standing about you. You do not see them because our world is determined by our senses. We can only see this outside. Let us call it X. We see that X according to our mental state. Let us take the tree standing outside. A thief came and what did he see in the stump? A policeman. The child saw a huge ghost. The young man was waiting for his sweetheart, and what did he see? His sweetheart. But the stump of the tree had not changed. It remained the same. This is God Himself, and with our foolishness we see Him to be man, to be dust, to be dumb, miserable.

Those who are similarly constituted will group together naturally and live in the same world. Otherwise stated, you live in the same place. All the heavens and all the hells are right here. For example: [take planes in the form of] big circles cutting each other at certain points. . . . On this plane in one circle we can be in touch with a certain point in another [circle]. If the mind gets to the centre, you begin to be conscious on all planes. In meditation sometimes you touch another plane, and you see other beings, disembodied spirits, and so on. You get there by the power of meditation. This power is changing our senses, you see, refining our senses. If you begin to practise meditation five days, you will feel the pain from within these centres [of conciousness] and hearing [becomes finer]. ... (See Complete Works, Vol. I). That is why all the Indian gods have three eyes. That is the psychic eye that opens out and shows you spiritual things.

As this power of Kundalini rises from one centre to the other in the spine, it changes the senses and you begin to see this world another. It is heaven. You cannot talk. Then the Kundalini goes down to the lower centres. You are again man until the Kundalini reaches the brain, all the centres have been passed, and the whole vision vanishes and you [perceive] . . . nothing but the one existence. You are God. All heavens you make out of Him, all worlds out of Him. He is the one existence. Nothing else exists.

The Practice Of Religion

(Delivered at Alameda, California, on April 18, 1900)*

We read many books, many scriptures. We get various ideas from our childhood, and change them every now and then. We understand what is meant by theoretical religion. We think we understand what is meant by practical religion. Now I am going to present to you my idea of practical religion.

We hear all around us about practical religion, and analysing all that, we find that it can be brought down to one conception — charity to our fellow beings. Is that all of religion? Every day we hear in this country about practical Christianity — that a man has done some good to his fellow beings. Is that all?

What is the goal of life? Is this world the goal of life? Nothing more? Are we to be just what we are, nothing more? Is man to be a machine which runs smoothly without a hitch anywhere? Are all the sufferings he experiences today all he can have, and doesn't he want anything more?

The highest dream of many religions is the world. ... The vast majority of people are dreaming of the time when there will be no more disease, sickness, poverty, or misery of any kind. They will have a good time all around. Practical religion, therefore, simply means. "Clean the streets! Make it nice!" We see how all enjoy it.

Is enjoyment the goal of life? Were it so, it would be a tremendous mistake to become a man at all. What man can enjoy a meal with more gusto than the dog or the cat ? Go to a menagerie and see the [wild animals] tearing the flesh from the bone. Go back and become a bird! . . . What a mistake then to become a man! Vain have been my years — hundreds of years — of struggle only to become the man of sense-enjoyments.

Mark, therefore, the ordinary theory of practical religion, what it leads to. Charity is great, but the moment you say it is all, you run the risk of running into materialism. It is not religion. It is no better than atheism - a little less. ... You Christians, have you found nothing else in the Bible than working for fellow creatures, building . . . hospitals ? . . . Here stands a shopkeeper and says how Jesus would have kept the shop! Jesus would neither have kept a saloon, nor a shop, nor have edited a newspaper. That sort of practical religion is good, not bad; but it is just kindergarten religion. It leads nowhere. . . . If you believe in God, if you are Christians and repeat everyday, "Thy will be done", just think what it means! You say every moment, "Thy will be done", really meaning, "My will be done by Thee, O God." The Infinite is working His own plans out. Even He has made mistakes, and you and I are going to remedy that! The Architect of the universe is going to be taught by the carpenters! He has left the world a dirty hole, and you are going to make it a beautiful place!

What is the goal of it all? Can senses ever be the goal? Can enjoyment of pleasure ever be the goal? Can this life ever be the goal of the soul? If it is, better die this moment; do not want this life! If that is the fate of man, that he is going to be only the perfected machine, it would just mean that we go back to being trees and stones and things like that. Did you ever hear a cow tell a lie or see a tree steal? They are perfect machines. They do not make mistakes. They live in a world where everything is finished. ...

What is the ideal of religion, then, if this cannot be practical [religion]? And it certainly cannot be. What are we here for? We are here for freedom, for knowledge. We want to know in order to make ourselves free. That is our life: one universal cry for freedom. What is the reason the . . . plant grows from the seed, overturning the ground and raising itself up to the skies? What is the offering for the earth from the sun? What is your life? The same struggle for freedom. Nature is trying all around to suppress us, and the soul wants to express itself. The struggle with nature is going on. Many things will be crushed and broken in this struggle for freedom. That is your real misery. Large masses of dust and dirt must be raised on the battlefield. Nature says, "I will conquer." The soul says, "I must be the conqueror." Nature says, "Wait! I will give you a little enjoyment to keep you quiet." The soul enjoys a little, becomes deluded a moment, but the next moment it [cries for freedom again]. Have you marked the eternal cry going on through the ages in every breast? We are deceived by poverty. We become wealthy and are deceived with wealth. We are ignorant. We read and learn and are deceived with knowledge. No man is ever satisfied. That is the cause of misery, but it is also the cause of all blessing. That is the sure sign. How can you be satisfied with this world? . . . If tomorrow this world becomes heaven, we will say, "Take this away. Give us something else."

The infinite human soul can never be satisfied but by the Infinite itself .... Infinite desire can only be satisfied by infinite knowledge — nothing short of that. Worlds will come and go. What of that? The soul lives and for ever expands. Worlds must come into the soul. Worlds must disappear in the soul like drops in the ocean. And this world to become the goal of the soul! If we have common sense, we cannot he satisfied, though this has been the theme of the poets in all the ages, always telling us to be satisfied. And nobody has been satisfied yet! Millions of prophets have told us, "Be satisfied with your lot"; poets sing. We have told ourselves to be quiet and satisfied, yet we are not. It is the design of the Eternal that there is nothing in this world to satisfy my soul, nothing in the heavens above, and nothing beneath. Before the desire of my soul, the stars and the worlds, upper and lower, the whole universe, is but a hateful disease, nothing but that. That is the meaning. Everything is an evil unless that is the meaning. Every desire is evil unless that is the meaning, unless you understand its true importance, its goal. All nature is crying through all the atoms for one thing — its perfect freedom.

What is practical religion, then? To get to that state — freedom, the attainment of freedom. And this world, if it helps us on to that goal, [is] all right; if not — if it begins to bind one more layer on the thousands already there, it becomes an evil. Possessions, learning, beauty, everything else — as long as they help us to that goal, they are of practical value. When they have ceased helping us on to that goal of freedom, they are a positive danger. What is practical religion, then? Utilise the things of this world and the next just for one goal — the attainment of freedom. Every enjoyment, every ounce of pleasure is to be bought by the expenditure of the infinite heart and mind combined.

Look at the sum total of good and evil in this world. Has it changed? Ages have passed, and practical religion has worked for ages. The world thought that each time the problem would be solved. It is always the same problem. At best it changes its form. ... It trades consumption and nerve disease for twenty thousand shops. . . . It is like old rheumatism: Drive it from one place, it goes to another. A hundred years ago man walked on foot or bought horses. Now he is happy because he rides the railroad; but he is unhappy because he has to work more and earn more. Every machine that saves labour puts more stress upon labour.

This universe, nature, or whatever you call it, must be limited; it can never be unlimited. The Absolute, to become nature, must be limited by time, space, and causation. The energy [at our disposal] is limited. You can spend it in one place, losing it in another. The sum total is always the same. Wherever there is a wave in one place, there is a hollow in another. If one nation becomes rich, others become poor. Good balances evil. The person for the moment on top of the wave thinks all is good; the person at the bottom says the world is [all evil]. But the man who stands aside sees the divine play going on. Some weep and others laugh. The latter will weep in their turn and the others laugh. What can we do ? We know we cannot do anything. ...

Which of us do anything because we want to do good? How few! They can be counted on the fingers. The rest of us also do good, but because we are forced to do so. ... We cannot stop. Onward we go, knocked about from place to place. What can we do? The world will be the same world, the earth the same. It will be changed from blue to brown and from brown to blue. One language translated into another, one set of evils changed into another set of evils — that is what is going on. ... Six of one, half a dozen of the other. The American Indian in the forest cannot attend a lecture on metaphysics as you can, but he can digest his meal. You cut him to pieces, and the next moment he is all right. You and I, if we get scratched, we have to go to the hospital for six months. ...

The lower the organism, the greater is its pleasure in the senses. Think of the lowest animals and the power of touch. Everything is touch. ... When you come to man, you will see that the lower the civilization of the man, the greater is the power of the senses. ... The higher the organism, the lesser is the pleasure of the senses. A dog can eat a meal, but cannot understand the exquisite pleasure of thinking about metaphysics. He is deprived of the wonderful pleasure which you get through the intellect. The pleasures of the senses are great. Greater than those is the pleasure of the intellect. When you attend the fine fifty-course dinner in Paris, that is pleasure indeed. But in the observatory, looking at the stars, seeing . . . worlds coming and developing — think of that! It must be greater, for I know you forget all about eating. That pleasure must be greater than what you get from worldly things. You forget all about wives, children, husbands, and everything; you forget all about the sense-plane. That is intellectual pleasure. It is common sense that it must be greater than sense pleasure. It is always for greater joy that you give up the lesser. This is practical religion — the attainment of freedom, renunciation. Renounce!

Renounce the lower so that you may get the higher. What is the foundation of society? Morality, ethics, laws. Renounce. Renounce all temptation to take your neighbour's property, to put hands upon your neighbour, all the pleasure of tyrannising over the weak, all the pleasure of cheating others by telling lies. Is not morality the foundation of society? What is marriage but the renunciation of unchastity? The savage does not marry.

Man marries because he renounces. So on and on. Renounce! Renounce! Sacrifice! Give up! Not for zero. Not for nothing. But to get the higher. But who can do this? You cannot, until you have got the higher. You may talk. You may struggle. You may try to do many things. But renunciation comes by itself when you have got the higher. Then the lesser falls away by itself.

This is practical religion. What else? Cleaning streets and building hospitals? Their value consists only in this renunciation. And there is no end to renunciation. The difficulty is they try to put a limit to it — thus far and no farther. But there is no limit to this renunciation.

Where God is, there is no other. Where the world is, there is no God. These two will never unite. [Like] light and darkness. That is what I have understood from Christianity and the life of the Teacher. Is not that Buddhism? Is not that Hinduism? Is not that Mohammedanism? Is not that the teaching of all the great sages and teachers? What is the world that is to be given up? It is here. I am carrying it all with me. My own body. It is all for this body that I put my hand voluntarily upon my fellow man, just to keep it nice and give it a little pleasure; [all for this body] that I injure others and make mistakes. ...

Great men have died. Weak men have died. Gods have died. Death — death everywhere. This world is a graveyard of the infinite past, yet we cling to this [body]: "I am never going to die". Knowing for sure [that the body must die] and yet clinging to it. There is meaning in that too [because in a sense we do not die]. The mistake is that we cling to the body when it is the spirit that is really immortal.

You are all materialists, because you believe that you are the body. If a man gives me a hard punch, I would say I am punched. If he strikes me, I would say I am struck. If I am not the body, why should I say so? It makes no difference if I *say* I am the spirit. I am the body just now. I have converted myself into matter. That is why I am to renounce the body, to go back to what I really am. I am the spirit — the soul no instrument can pierce, no sword can cut asunder, no fire can burn, no air can dry. Unborn and uncreated, without beginning and without end, deathless, birthless and omnipresent — that is what I am; and all misery comes just because I think this little lump of clay is myself. I am identifying myself with matter and taking all the consequences.

Practical religion is identifying myself with my Self. Stop this wrong identification! How far are you advanced in that? You may have built two thousand hospitals, built fifty thousand roads, and yet what of that, if you, have not realised that you are the spirit? You die a dog's; death, with the same feelings that the dog does. The dog howls and weeps because he knows that he is only matter and he is going to be dissolved.

There is death, you know, inevitable death, in water, in air, in the palace, in the prison - death everywhere. What makes you fearless? When you have realised what you are — that infinite spirit, deathless, birthless. Him no fire can burn, no instrument kill, no poison hurt. Not theory, mind you. Not reading books. . . . [Not parroting.] My old Master used to say, "It is all very good to teach the parrot to say, 'Lord, Lord, Lord' all the time; but let the cat come and take hold of its neck, it forgets all about it" [You may] pray all the time, read all the scriptures in the world, and worship all the gods there are, [but] unless you realise the soul there is no freedom. Not talking, theorising, argumentation, but realisation. That I call practical religion.

This truth about the soul is first to be heard. If you have heard it, think about it. Once you have done that, meditate upon it. No more vain arguments! Satisfy yourself once that you are the infinite spirit. If that is true, it must be nonsense that you are the body. You are the Self, and that must be realised. Spirit must see itself as spirit. Now the spirit is seeing itself as body. That must stop. The moment you begin to realise that, you are released.

You see this glass, and you know it is simply an illusion. Some scientists tell you it is light and vibration. ... Seeing the spirit must be infinitely more real: than that, must be the only true state, the only true sensation, the only true vision. All these [objects you see], are but dreams. You know that now. Not the old idealists alone, but modern physicists also tell you that light is there. A little more vibration makes all the difference. ...

You must see God. The spirit must be realised, and that is practical religion. It is not what Christ preached that *you* call practical religion: "Blessed are the poor in spirit for theirs is the Kingdom of Heaven." Was it a joke? What is the practical religion you are thinking, of? Lord help us! "Blessed are the pure in heart, for they shall see God." That means street-cleaning, hospital-building, and all that? Good works, when you do them with a pure mind. Don't give the man twenty dollars and buy all the papers in San Francisco to see your name! Don't you read in your own books how no man will help you? Serve as worship of the Lord Himself in the poor, the miserable, the weak. That done, the result is secondary. That sort of work, done without any thought of gain, benefits the soul. And even of such is the Kingdom of Heaven.

The Kingdom of Heaven is within us. He is there. He is the soul of all souls. See Him in your own soul. That is practical religion. That is freedom. Let us ask each other how much we are advanced in that: how much we are worshippers of the body, or real believers in God, the spirit; how much we believe ourselves to be spirit. That is selfless. That is freedom. That is real worship. Realise yourself. That is all there is to do. Know yourself as you are — infinite spirit. That is practical religion. Everything else is impractical, for everything else will vanish. That alone will never vanish. It Is eternal. Hospitals will tumble down. Railroad givers will all die. This earth will be blown to pieces, suns wiped out. The soul endureth for ever.

Which is higher, running after these things which perish or. . . . worshipping that which never changes? Which is more practical, spending all the energies of life in getting things, and before you have got them death comes and you have to leave them all? — like the great [ruler] who conquered all, [who when] death came, said, "Spread out all the jars of things before me." He said "Bring me that big diamond." And he placed it on his breast and wept. Thus weeping, he died the same as the dog dies.

Man says, "I live." He knows not that it is [the fear of] death that makes him cling slavishly to life. He says "I enjoy." He never dreams that nature has enslaved him.

Nature grinds all of us. Keep count of the ounce of pleasure you get. In the long run, nature did her work through you, and when you die your body will make other plants grow. Yet we think all the time that we are getting pleasure ourselves. Thus the wheel goes round.

Therefore to realise the spirit as spirit is practical religion. Everything else is good so far as it leads to this one grand idea. That [realization] is to be attained by renunciation, by meditation — renunciation of all the senses, cutting the knots, the chains that bind us down to matter. "I do not want to get material life, do not want the sense-life, but something higher." That is renunciation. Then, by the power of meditation, undo the mischief that has been done.

We are at the beck and call of nature. If there is sound outside, I have to hear it. If something is going on, I have to see it. Like monkeys. We are two thousand monkeys concentrated, each one of us. Monkeys are very curious. So we cannot help ourselves, and call this "enjoying". Wonderful this language! We are enjoying the world! We cannot help enjoying it. Nature wants us to do it. A beautiful sound: I am hearing it. As if I could choose to hear it or not! Nature says, "Go down to the depths of misery." I become miserable in a moment. ... We talk about pleasures [of the senses] and possessions. One man thinks me very learned. Another thinks, "He is a fool." This degradation, this slavery, without knowing anything! In the dark room we are knocking our heads against each other.

What is meditation? Meditation is the power which enables us to resist all this. Nature may call us, "Look there is a beautiful thing!" I do not look. Now she says, "There is a beautiful smell; smell it! " I say to my nose, "Do not smell it", and the nose doesn't. "Eyes, do not see!" Nature does such an awful thing - kills one of my children, and says, "Now, rascal, sit down and weep! Go to the depths!" I say, "I don't have to." I jump up. I must be free. Try it sometimes. ... [In meditation], for a moment, you can change this nature. Now, if you had that power in yourself, would not that be heaven, freedom? That is the power of meditation.

How is it to be attained? In a dozen different ways. Each temperament has its own way. But this is the general principle: get hold of the mind. The mind is like a lake, and every stone that drops into it raises waves. These waves do not let us see what we are. The full moon is reflected in the water of the lake, but the surface is so disturbed that we do not see the reflection clearly. Let it be calm. Do not let nature raise the wave. Keep quiet, and then after a little while she will give you up. Then we know what we are. God is there already, but the mind is so agitated, always running after the senses. You close the senses and [yet] you whirl and whirl about. Just this moment I think I am all right and I will meditate upon God, and then my mind goes to London in one minute. And if I pull it away from there, it goes to New York to think about the things I have done there in the past. These [waves] are to be stopped by the power of meditation.

Slowly and gradually we are to train ourselves. It is no joke — not a question of a day, or years, or maybe of births. Never mind! The pull must go on. Knowingly, voluntarily, the pull must go on. Inch by inch we will gain ground. We will begin to feel and get real possessions, which no one can take away from us — the wealth that no man can take, the wealth that nobody can destroy, the joy that no misery can hurt any more. ...

All these years we have depended upon others. If I have a little pleasure and that person goes away, my pleasure is gone. ... See the folly of man: he depends for happiness upon men! All separations are misery.

Naturally. Depending upon wealth for happiness? There is fluctuation of wealth. Depending upon health or upon anything except the unchangeable spirit must bring misery today or tomorrow.

Excepting the infinite spirit, everything else is changing. There is the whirl of change. Permanence is nowhere except in yourself. There is the infinite joy, unchanging. Meditation is the gate that opens that to us. Prayers, ceremonials, and all the other forms of worship are simply kindergartens of meditation. You pray, you offer something. A certain theory existed that everything raised one's spiritual power. The use of certain words, flowers, images, temples, ceremonials like the waving of lights brings the mind to that attitude, but that attitude is always in the human soul, nowhere else. [People] are all doing it; but what they do without knowing it, do knowingly. That is the power of meditation. All knowledge you have — how did it come? From the power of meditation. The soul churned the knowledge out of its own depths. What knowledge was there ever outside of it? In the long run this power of meditation separates ourselves from the body, and then the soul knows itself as it is — the unborn, the deathless, and birthless being. No more is there any misery, no more births upon this earth, no more evolution. [The soul knows itself as having] ever been perfect and free.